INDIA
AND
WORLD
CULTURE

INDIA AND WORLD CULTURE

VINAYAK KRISHNA GOKAK

VIKAS PUBLICATIONS

DELHI ● BOMBAY ● BANGALORE
KANPUR ● LONDON

VIKAS PUBLICATIONS

5 Daryaganj, Ansari Road, Delhi-6
Savoy Chambers, 5 Wallace Street, Bombay-1
10 First Main Road, Gandhi Nagar, Bangalore-9
80 Canning Road, Kanpur
17-21 Sunbeam Road, North Acton, London N.W. 10

SBN 7069 0175 4

162714

301.2954

G616I

PRINTED IN INDIA

AT INDRAPRASTHA PRESS, NEHRU HOUSE, BAHADUR SHAH ZAFAR MARG,
NEW DELHI-1, AND PUBLISHED BY MRS SHARDA CHAWLA, VIKAS
PUBLICATIONS, 5 DARYAGANJ, ANSARI ROAD, DELHI-6

Preface

I planned this book during my first year at the Indian Institute of Advanced Study, Simla. A good part of the material used in Chapters VI and VIII was prepared for certain occasions at the Institute. The invitations extended by the Bharatiya Vidya Bhavan and the Andhra and Poona Universities to deliver a series of endowment lectures provided me the opportunity to prepare the material included of Chapters V, VII, and X and part of the material of Chapter IV. A national broadcast on the AIR and the felicitation volume to be offered to Dr P.B. Gajendragadkar enabled me to think out part of the material presented in Chapters III and IX. I am grateful to all the authorities concerned for having given me opportunities which helped me to plan and write this book.

It is not as though the book arose out of these occasions and lectures. These latter enabled me to write the book that I had been long wanting to write.

Being neither a historian nor an anthropologist, I do not present this book as a study in either field. As a lover of culture, it has been my endeavour to understand what culture is and what the Indian pattern, to which I myself belong, looks like. I present my findings in this book with such understanding and insight as I possess as a student of literature and linguistics and as a man of letters.

I planned this book as a tribute to Sri Aurobindo on the

occasion of his birth centenary. Indeed, the reader will easily see that practically every chapter in the book is an application or amplification of Sri Aurobindo's insights on the subject.

Brindavan, Whitefield,   VINAYAK KRISHNA GOKAK
Bangalore

Contents

TO

SRI AUROBINDO
kindler of new horizons and destinies
during the year of his birth centenary

1

Towards a Definition of Culture

Culture is, no doubt, a comprehensive term. Dr Julian Huxley, then Executive Secretary of the Preparatory Commission for UNESCO, who put forward the idea of the UNESCO Publication, *History of Mankind,* in 1946, wrote:

> The chief task before the Humanities today would seem to be to help in constructing a history of the development of the human mind, notably in its highest cultural achievements. For this task, the help of art critics and artists will be needed as well as of art historians; of anthropologists and students of comparative religion as well as of divines and theologians; of archaeologists as well as of classical scholars; of poets and creative men of letters as well as of professors of literature; as well as the whole-hearted support of the historians.

It is well known that the anthropologists, who claim to have culture as their special field of study, are themselves not agreed on the connotation of the word. Anthropologists like Weber and MacIver are inclined to make a distinction between culture and civilization, restricting civilization to science and technology and culture to philosophy, religion, and the arts. But

Kroeber uses the word "culture" as the customary term applicable alike to high or low products of societies. "Civilization" is used as a term for the larger and richer cultures, carrying an overtone of high development of a specific society.

I am inclined to accept Kroeber's definition of "civilization" as "the historically differentiated and variable mass of customary ways of functioning of human societies", because of its comprehensiveness. He analyzes the components of culture at three levels: basic culture, social culture, and value culture. He pleads that this classification is only a conceptual axis which facilitates understanding and is bound to be capricious, if pushed too far. He himself posits language as a fourth component, morality and law as a fifth, and fashion as a sixth component. This is a good enough framework for an analytical presentation.

What I am concerned with here is "value culture" or "fine culture". The common man has this in mind when he speaks of "culture". It means the value-system of the individual, his scale of values and also the national pattern of culture to which he himself belongs. In this sense, culture is the pursuit of perfection in life. Powys describes culture as creative self-sculpture. Perfection may always remain an unrealized ideal because there may be various levels in perfection too. The Duke of Windsor, when he was Prince of Wales, seems to have remarked: "Culture? It's a fine idea. I wish man will be able to realize it some day."

It is not growing like a tree that makes a man cultured. Age by itself is no criterion of culture. Culture does not necessarily consist in an intense attachment to any idea or doctrine. An attachment of this kind may generate fanaticism but not culture. In these days of increasing specialization, one cannot say that a specialist or an expert in a narrow field of knowledge is necessarily a cultured man. Expertise in a subject does not

2

always go with culture. The uncultured man, as Powys said, displays his ideas lightly like a man who jingles the few coins he has in his pocket.

Culture implies the pursuit of perfection in all walks of life. It was Matthew Arnold who spoke of the pursuit of perfection fulfilling itself in two ways: the Hellenism of the Greeks and the Hebraism of the Jews. Hellenism, according to Arnold, denotes the spontaneity of consciousness and Hebraism the strictness of conscience. One stresses delight, heart-ease or *ananda* and the other the ethical aspect: purity of conduct, *tapasya* or askesis. If culture is the pursuit of perfection, it stands for perfection in purity of thought, feeling as well as deed. A cultured man is the integrated man. He is not divided within himself and against himself. He has overcome this self-division. An unevolved individual suffers continuously from self-division. His words belie his deeds and his thoughts his feelings. On the other hand, a cultured man's thoughts, feelings, and deeds are in harmony with each other. He achieves, in his own personality, a happy synthesis of knowledge, works and nobility of feeling. Like Wordsworth's happy warrior, a cultured man unites in his own personality the twin phases of action and contemplation. Like the bee that Swift, and later Matthew Arnold spoke of, he compasses the two ends of sweetness and light in his own being.

Culture, therefore, consists in a harmonious and balanced cultivation of all the faculties in man: intellect and emotion, intuition and sense perception, flesh as well as spirit. Nero, the Roman emperor, had a perverted mind. His hunger for unusual sights, quite apart from their moral or even human implications, made him a neurotic and sadist. Cleopatra was too much plunged in the life of the senses to be regarded as a cultured lady. She became all "air and fire" only when Antony died and she realized the futility of physical passion.

3

This is at least true of Shakespeare's Cleopatra. An undue attachment to a life of spirit can also lead to lack of culture. Tagore's *Sanyasi* spent twenty to thirty years in the Himalayas, practising penance, and felt that he had attained the Divine. But he discovered, to his utter horror, that, on his return a simple beggar girl aroused in him an overwhelming emotion, giving the lie to his impressions that all such emotions had been extinguished within him. The ascetic's denial betrays as much lack of culture as the sensualist's entanglement with the senses. A wrongly felt intuition can lead to hasty and impulsive and, therefore, uncultured action as illustrated by the hero of W.B. Yeats' *The Unicorn From The Stars*.

However great an artist may be, uncontrolled emotion is sure to demonstrate his lack of culture. Strindberg, the great dramatist, for example, used to go mad whenever his cooks forsook him. An excessive reliance on the intellect may also lead to an unhealthy attitude in life. One may become a cynic and live life in a manner utterly devoid of taste or joy. There is a Sanskrit verse which points out that human beings are like pieces of wood adrift at sea. They float together for a while and then get separated. This may be true. At the same time, even a moment of companionship can be enduring and as full of joy as eternity. Browning gives a fine picture of this state of experience in his poem *The Last Ride Together*. The cynic loses the beauty and harmony which reside in an emotional and intuitive approach to life.

Neglect or carelessness even in the observance of minor rules of health or conduct may reveal a proportionate lack of culture in highly gifted men. Gandhiji has narrated in his autobiography, how Gopal Krishna Gokhale, who was regarded by him as his political *guru*, never took any physical exercise. It was this neglect of health that brought about his premature end. But to make a fetish of one's health also means taking to a bye-lane which may or may not have the stamp of culture on it. There is a story woven round Gorakhnath who was an adept in *hatayoga* and excelled in many endurance tests and feats. When he met another saint, Allama Prabhu, Gorakhnath offered Prabhu a sword, challenging Prabhu to kill Gorakhnath, if he could. Allama struck with all his vehemence and the sword glanced back, hardly touching Gorakhnath's skin, as if it had been flourished against a flint. But Allama offered the same sword to Gorakhnath inviting him to strike at Allama Prabhu with it. When Gorakhnath tried to cut Prabhu's body into two, the sword passed through the body as if through air and the two separated halves were united again, like air itself. Culture, which is perfect in all its parts, is like air rather than earth. One can specialize and master a particular craft or discipline; but the cultured man is as unattached and as universal as air.

Even a mystic, who is not actively aware of his own time and place and is lost in his brooding on eternity, does not fit into our definition of culture. He may be of all time. But he has to belong to his own time and place and contribute actively to the progress and well-being of his fellowmen, if he is to be regarded as a cultured person.

This brings us to the consideration of an adequate formula for defining the cultured man. Culture implies an integrated personality and neither time nor eternity can be left out of it. The cultured man reconciles the universal with the particular and the claims of time with the claims of eternity. Taine, the French literary historian, spoke of the race, the moment, and the milieu as factors determining the form and substance of literary history in a given epoch. But he left out an all-important factor: the personality of the individual. The human personality, as sages and prophets have proved on their own pulses, can rise to any level of perception or consciousness, hardly dreamed of by others. But this perception also has to reckon with the three other factors, if the individual is to function in the spirit of true culture. It is likely that each one of these factors may lead to deviation or distortion in one or the other way, if it is turned into a hobby horse and pursued in excess. To take a few instances from literary history, Kipling's writings were frequently disfigured by his sense of racial pride. There came into his poetry a jingoistic note which detracted considerably from its enduring significance. As for environment, one has to judge whether conformity to or revolt against it is justified from the point of view of culture. Pandit Malaviyaji, an orthodox Hindu who modelled his behaviour on what the scriptures, even the apocryphal scriptures, said, set them side and went to England for the Round Table Conference in spite of the fact that orthodoxy banned journeys across the seas. Gandhiji, who cared only for truth and even put it far above the freedom of India, rode on the crest of the wave, caught the Time Spirit by its forelock and launched the movement of non-violent non-cooperation against the British because that moment in the life of the nation needed it.

If one were to speak of men of letters who realized this ideal of culture in their own lives, one could mention Kalidasa and Shakespeare. They belonged to their age but they also were of all time. The poetry of Kalidasa is a vivid portrayal of the problems, the pressures, the glory, and the splendour of the Gupta period. But it also sets forth the eternal verities in an unmistakable manner. Shakespeare's plays fulfil themselves in a similar way. The entire Elizabethan England can be found in his plays. At the same time his heroes and heroines are types and individuals that can be met with in all countries in any age.

The cultured man is not just interested in perfecting himself. He also helps to perfect the world because his passion for perfection does not end only with himself. Culture may be an end in itself. But the very fact that a person is cultured makes its own contribution to the society around him. Viewed nationally, culture is a means to an end, the end being the happiness and all-round prosperity of one's own country and of humanity.

Philosophy and religion, the fine arts, Nature, love and friendship are some of the channels which can irrigate human lives and lead to a worldwide harvest of culture. If the philosopher, the man of religion, the artist and poet are not men of culture, at least in the creative springs of their personality, their writings will not make for the diffusion of culture. One has therefore to be careful in surrendering oneself to any specific philosophy or work of art. It may be that some of the limitations of the artist or the thinker project themselves into his work. The impassioned prose of Nietzsche was full of power and energy. But along with power and movement, there was no adequate measure of light. The light available was obscured by the turbidity of his impulsiveness. The result was that Nietzsche sowed the wind and reaped the whirlwind called Hitler.

A love of Nature, truth and friendship, and the company of the good and great can diffuse the authentic values of culture effectively. These are the graces of life that contribute substantially to the greatness of a civilization.

The coming generation may do well to remember that action alone is not the *summun bonum* of life. Macbeth, the villian-hero of Shakespeare's great tragedy, acted impulsively and spent the rest of his life in desperate repentance. On the other hand, Hamlet lived a life of utter indecision and by the time he was inclined to act, it was too late. Thought, feeling, and action have to blossom simultaneously, like three roses on a stem, and express the root-intuition of the complete personality. If precedence has to be given till this becomes possible, it will have to go to intensive thinking and deep feeling. An agility of judgment, changing as new facts come into our ken, a purity of feeling, which is untainted by any preference or prejudice, and a readiness to act to the extent necessary without fear or favour, once the decision is made, are the sure marks of a cultured personality fully formed or in the making.

It is now clear that there can be no foreground without its background relief, no effective specialization unless it is backed up by a wide, fundamental knowledge of other departments of thought and of life and reality. Book-worms can be boring. But subject-worms run the risk of being dehumanized, becoming efficient tools and, for that very reason, lifeless or insensitive to the beauty and movement of life.

Lastly, the contemplation of eternity should not obscure the vision of the social scene animated and active all around us. Nor should our complete absorption in the social scene make us oblivious of the verities that abide long after our lips are dumb and our hands and feet are clay. For, after all,

We are such stuff
As dreams are made on and our little life
Is rounded with a sleep.

2

Culture and Society

When Matthew Arnold spoke of the barbarian, the philistine, and the populace, and divided the English society of his time into these three classes, he was looking for signs and traces of culture with a great deal of scepticism and frustration. The rich man who does not care for culture; the middle class man who is satisfied with his narrow successes, and thinks, in his self-importance, that there is nothing else worth acquiring; and the populace which is struggling all the time for mere subsistence, having hardly any time for the finer things of life: if these are the persons that constitute the society, how can there be any scope for culture? The dissemination or diffusion of culture presupposes that man is above want; that he has not to struggle for food and shelter; and that the prevalence of law and the dispensation of justice in society are assured. It is difficult for culture to flourish, if we have to fight for our daily bread. Any cultural system that does not satisfy these requirements is bound to be partial or fragmentary. The culture of ancient India, Greece, and Rome was a partial culture. It was restricted, in many ways, to one class of people. One can say about their culture what Tennyson said about Sir Lancelot:

His honour rooted in dishonour stood
And faith unfaithful kept him falsely true

The French and Russian revolutions were upsurges against the fragmentariness and exclusiveness of a culture of this kind. The scene in India is changing today for similar reasons. The struggle for power, the bid for white-collar jobs, and the frantic pursuit of security are all off-shoots of this desire for a universal diffusion of culture. The struggle for wealth and power is relentless because it is assumed that cultured life is impossible without such a foundation.

How then shall we make sure that a universal diffusion of culture becomes possible? In the first place, each individual has to be assured of his absolute security and his full dignity in the society he lives in. This means that an egalitarian society, whether it is made possible through a capitalist, socialist or Marxist initiative, comes into being. Secondly, the security and comfort of an affluent society should not send a person to sleep. Leisure has no value for one who does not know how to use it. The pursuit of culture depends on the availability of leisure. But it also presupposes an intense desire for culture, a passion for perfection. If the common man in Japan spends his spare time on *pachungo* and the aristocrat on playing bridge, there can be no hope for culture. Leisure is bound to be misused by the common man if a deep and steady aspiration for the finer things of life is not implanted in him right from the beginning. This means that our educational system must be overhauled so as to promote the cultural urge in each pupil at home and school. In saying this, we assume that there is an atmosphere of culture in the family and that teachers are available who can inspire in the young this passion for perfection from their childhood. The whole question then turns upon the action of individuals, the individuals that compose a family or run a school.

The attempt to diffuse culture on a universal scale is a long and arduous undertaking. Perhaps the Indian sages were right when they assumed that all human beings could not be said to have reached the same stage of evolution. There are manifold evolutionary steps. For one reason or the other, and by virtue of the temperament with which they are endowed, human beings move at different stages of the journey. The idea of the four *varnas* or categories of human beings was therefore conceived as a code of conduct for each one of these categories. Duties were prescribed according to the capacities and inclinations of each category within a religious framework. It is tragic that the principle of heredity gradually distorted and falsified this idea.

A great deal of bitterness has been caused in recent times by the very mention of the phrase *chatur varnas*. The petrification of the *varnas* into a system of castes and creeds and the recognition of social rank and position according to birth cannot be condemned too severely. But the four *varnas* or types characterize human society in all parts of the world. The thinker, the warrior, the purveyor, and the worker typify four kinds or levels of human activity and all of them are essential for the maintenance of society. A progressive society gives equal opportunities to all to prove their worth and aptitude and assigns to each individual the vocation for which he is fitted. We have yet to realize the value of this great truth in a caste-ridden society like ours. Mere variety, without the controlling principle of unity, results in chaos. Almost every religious revival in India vivisected the country further by adding one more sect to the numerous castes and creeds that already existed. Sectarianism could know no end when the living centre of national consciousness was itself dormant.

Unless there is a background of social and cultural unity to this diversity of castes and creeds and even of political parties in the nation, a structural disintegration may confront our society. The nation must be held together socially and culturally, if it is to be called upon to preserve the multitude of castes and creeds and judge a variety of political issues and programmes. Indian culture has always been instinct with this sense of unity. This sense of unity has to be disengaged from ancient, medieval and modern accretions and reasserted in the midst of a changing world order.

We live in a chaotic age that is full of contradictions and confusions. We struggle to survive in an era of strikes and other forms of labour unrest when capitalism itself has hardly been able to fulfil the constructive role which Marx assigned to it in *Das Capital*. The advanced countries tend to dominate developing countries, directly or indirectly. Several forms of human misery have been eliminated from some parts of the world. But other forms of it have cropped up in our push-button era. In an age pulsating with contradictory ideologies, it has become very difficult for a person to choose his own path of evolution.

The message of the Buddha bears a great relevance to these problems of our contemporary world. The Buddha preached the gospel of liberty, equality, and fraternity far more meaningfully than the French Revolution did. Though he was not sure of the complete elimination of human misery in the foreseeble future, he advocated compassion which can at least do a great deal to relieve it. Wherever he saw an open conflict between reason and religion, he stressed the need for a scientific and open-eyed approach to spiritual fulfilment. He stood for liberty in the highest sense of the term so that an individual could rise to his own highest stature, going beyond the life of the senses and intellect and climbing into an ineffable transcendence. As for the gospel of equality, he turned his back on the seventh heaven itself and affirmed that he would have nothing to do with it till the last human being was saved from ignorance and bondage. The world was, for the Buddha, a *sangha*, a fraternity, whose sovereignty the individual had to accept if he aspired to exceed himself.

India is now overhauling the structure of its society in order to remould it in the light of such an ideal. From this point of view, the secularism, which India has adopted as the sheet-anchor of its social and cultural policy, is indeed a significant philosophy. Secularism can be described as a religion without any religiosity in it. While permitting every individual perfect freedom of belief and conviction, it requires him, as a social unit, to fulfil certain obligations towards the society of which he is a member. Birth is no criterion of worth. He alone is competent who proves his competence by what he thinks, says, or does. No one has the right to inflict injury on others. The *dhoti* and the pyjama, the long coat and the short coat, not to speak of the petticoat, have all of them, their equal rights before the law, provided the minimum decency is observed. Each man is free to elect his own mode of worship and living.

The factors which foment social differences in India are now being opposed. Each religion has been assured proper protection while no religion can afford to be aggressive. Each language can grow to its full stature on the lines determined by its own genius. But no single language can strangle or overwhelm another. The liquidation of the zamindari system and of the feudal order of princes and the shift of emphasis, with regard to government servants, on their work as servants of the public as distinguished from their position as bureaucrats, are sure to take us a long way on the road to equality and liberty. The real challenge to our democracy today is casteism and communalism. But with the rapid spread of education, this too may be a discarded shibboleth.

The social reformer, who is at work in our midst, sometimes proposes drastic remedies which are worse than the disease itself.

13

Intercommunal marriage is thus frequently upheld as the one panacea for all communal differences. A kind of social regimentation is sought to be imposed upon what is essentially the problem of the individual. Marriage is an intensely personal affair. The fact that man is the architect of his own fortune or misfortune is nowhere better borne out than with regard to marriage. The alliances which used to be arranged in the past between royal families on political grounds deserve as much to be condemned as the marriages which are sought to be promoted today for reasons of social unity. If a love marriage is intercommunal, a progressive society is bound to welcome it. But to arrange a marriage on intercommunal lines as a weapon against communalism is to exploit the individual in the interest of an irrelevant social idea. Such a step can hardly have the desired effect. Instead of promoting social reconciliation, it may as well pave the way for another irreconcilable community.

The real basis of reconciliation lies in the core of human kindliness and tolerance. It has only to be awakened in order to be brought to the forefront. Even today, in the villages, the Hindus and the Muslims live together in perfect amity and respect each other's religion and religious habits, without the Hindu becoming a Muslim or the Muslim a Hindu. We frequently find in our towns and villages families belonging to different communities living on the friendliest terms, without discarding their own habits and customs. A day may come when the barriers between communities will fall and all will adopt a universal code of conduct. But it is certain that any compulsion or regimentation towards hastening the dawn of such a day will only end in delaying it further. The great and sure remedy lies not in converting the other man to our fold, caste or creed. It does not also consist in a drastic negation of all such differences. It lies in revolutionizing our own outlook, in changing vision, and in seeing the other man as we see ourselves.

14

Man has to take his stand, not on his egoistic self, but on his psyche which makes the whole world kin. He will then be able to feel the pulse of humanity and see steadily and whole, approaching the essential human values which lie masked under the heavy weight of custom and communal habit. Seen in this light, secularism is what Tagore called "The Religion of Man". It is the credo of Sri Aurobindo's *vishwa manava*.

At a time when there is a wrong insistence on religion, caste, and creed, secularism, which is only a negative attitude, assumes positive significance. It is the stream of clear reason which washes away all impurities of mind and heart. Later, secularism has to be supplemented by innate psychic insight, by that primal human sympathy of which Wordsworth spoke. When we have assimilated the lower aspects of secularism, we shall be ripe for the next transformation. Secularism is thus the great healer of social differences. It is the integral approach that reconciles opposites.

When the social structure of our national life is founded on this basis, it will be possible to project this attitude actively on the international plane. I remember an amusing incident about an Indian couple who went to Germany for a holiday. They did not know a word of German. But a German couple that met them smiled to them in a kindly way and spoke to them through man's first language—the language of gestures. They signalled to the Indian couple as if to ask them whether they were husband and wife. On receiving a nod in the affirmative, the German couple pointed to the Indians' fingers and asked them why they did not have the marriage ring. The Indians did not have the marriage rings on at that time. They admitted as much. Then the German gentleman pointed to the heart suggesting that, when hearts were one, marriage rings did not matter at all.

This incident, I venture to think, brings us to the heart of the matter. It is the heart that matters and not the ring, the language, the creed, or the community which belongs to one or to which one belongs. Belongings are mere trappings. It is the soul of man that makes him nobly human. We have seen how soldiers fighting on opposite sides, when the two World Wars were on, felt towards each other like brothers, while lying wounded side by side. In the communal riots that followed in the wake of August 1947, we have known of Hindu families harbouring Muslim refugees at great risk to themselves and vice versa. The greater the difficulty, the greater is the spirit that man displays. One can only hope that a well-planned system of national education will awaken the soul in every individual and build here a new society on imperishable foundations.

I cannot do better than conclude this chapter with a few lines from Sri Aurobindo. These lines are to be found in Canto I, Book XI, of *Savitri*:

> *Then in the process of evolving Time*
> *All shall be drawn into a single plan,*
> *A divine harmony shall be earth's law,*
> *Beauty and Joy remould her way to live....*
> *The Spirit shall be the master of this world*
> *Lurking no more in form's obscurity*
> *And Nature shall reverse her action's rule,*
> *The outward world disclose the Truth it veils.*
> *Even should a hostile force cling to its reign*
> *And claim its right's perpetual sovereignty*
> *And man refuse his high spiritual fate,*
> *Yet shall the secret Truth in things prevail.*
> *For in the march of all-fulfilling Time*
> *The hour must come of the Transcendent's will:*
> *All turns and winds towards His predestined ends*
> *In nature's fixed inevitable course*
> *Decreed since the beginning of the worlds*
> *In the deep essence of created things.*

3

Science and Culture

Science is important for determining the cultural pattern of an age or country. The scientist is busy making a bid for conquering space and solving the riddles posed by time. Science has relegated ancient pantheons to the anthropomorphic lumber-room and has been unable to perceive the mystical and psychological significance of these pantheons. Science has functioned like a minor Jesus, producing miraculous cures for diseases which, for a long time, were regarded incurable. But applied science, which ushered in eras of industrialism and technology and all the marvels of space exploration, has also confronted humanity with numerous other diseases. It has created as many problems as it has helped to solve. It is true that all higher life will be crippled if it is not supported by material well-being. But an undue stress on materialism may bring about economic barbarism in the absence of controlling mental and moral ideas.

Another significance of science consists in its insistence on the cultivation of reason and experimental observation. This is a vital factor in any cultural pattern and individuals will turn obscurantists if reason is not given its proper place in the cultivation of a balanced personality. When Indians lost their hold on reason and abandoned themselves indiscriminately to subtleties of spiritual life, they opened the door to all possible calamities and disintegrating forces. If the scientist dismisses all pantheons as anthropomorphic lumber-rooms, the indiscriminating believer tends to worship even evil spirits. Reason is, as Sri Aurobindo said, a good servant, but a bad master. Reason cannot appropriate to itself the right to an exclusive perception of reality. There are other aspects of life which reason cannot possibly perceive. The dialectic of the heart, of which Goethe spoke, and the field of intuitive perception are areas which reason can well define vividly, but not perceive in its own right. An undue stress on reason may bring about a resurgence of barbarism under cover of a utilitarian civilization.

It is worth remembering that scientific generalizations are short-lived though the facts of science themselves may be reliable. In the field of generalizations, Galileo cancelled Copernicus and Einstein cancelled Newton. It has been held, for instance, that the ape-kind developed into man. But this is purely speculative. It is quite possible that a type resembling the ape, but characteristic of itself and not of apehood, may have developed and become man. The evolutionists hold that life can affect matter and mind affect life. This may be conceded. But there is no proof that matter developed into life and life into mind or that a cabbage became a monkey and a monkey a man.

What we need is integral knowledge. It is not always true to say that the senses and reason go together. Our own sense perception tells us, as Sri Aurobindo points out, that the earth is flat. But science distinguishes reality from sense reality and suggests that the earth is approximately round. Science can therefore contradict the senses in certain fields.

Some scientists treat matter as the sole reality. But matter is now known as the structure of energy and its motions may be, in the words of Sri Aurobindo, steps of a secret consciousness. Life, mind, and spirit are other realities and we need to know them if we are interested in a total comprehension.

It has been held that the analytical methods of science are the only methods by which reality can be perceived as it is. These methods are, no doubt, effective. We must isolate an object before we know how to classify it. There are, as Sri Aurobindo remarks, three characteristics that distinguish an object: individuality, commonalty, and essentiality. We can know an object in its totality only when we have apprehended these three characteristics. Thus a diamond is a diamond, and a pearl a pearl. This is individuality. A diamond is real and not an illusion. But if we have knowledge and control of the elements and the common properties of the class of diamonds and pearls, we can make either a diamond or a pearl at our pleasure. The category represented by diamonds or pearls has first to be mastered. By mastering the category and its properties, we can produce the object that belongs to that type or category. Again, all matter is energy or motion manifested as substance. If we master this essentiality of matter, we can even arrive at the power of transmutation and transmute one metal into another.

The law of contradiction ceases to hold good in a more dramatic manner when we go higher than the material plane. Think of man, for instance. A human being has his own individuality, his commonalty as a particular member of the human race, and his essentiality if we judge him by the soul in him or by the extent to which he expresses the absolute in his own personality. This last makes him one in spirit with other human beings.

Reality is indivisible. We must avoid the initial analytical error if we have to grasp the nature of reality. It is true that the tree evolves out of the seed and vice versa. But this law

19

explains the process, a continuation of genes in particular modes, and not the mystery itself of the tree. The formula H_2O explains the process by which water comes into being. But the mystery of water itself is not explained. The separate law governing the evolution of an object is only an extension of the universal law of nature. The tree does not explain the seed nor the seed the tree. To quote Sri Aurobindo again, cosmos explains both and God explains cosmos.

There is a creative power which organizes various levels of reality. The atom or electron is the unit for the organization of matter. These inifinitesimals are charged with an immense energy and their association by design results in the formation of earth, metals, and so on. At the level of life, the living cell is created as a unit, an original plasm that is multiplied. At the level of mind, man manifests mind with the ego as a unit. The evolutionary difference between one level and another has to be explained, not by the outer process of transition, but by the manifestation of a creative power according to different principles.

Science has yet to tackle these various levels of reality in the total range of existence. The mystics have perceived levels higher than mind itself. The parapsychologist is trying to explore some of the phenomena on one of these levels. The modern psychologist is busy sizing up the lower levels of consciousness—the unconscious and subconscious. He has some awareness of the subliminal consciousness but he has yet to reckon with what Sri Aurobindo called the psychic and super-conscient awareness.

Sociology works today on the basis of certain new tendencies created in the West: vitalistic egoism and collectivism. These tendencies were responsible for Nietzsche's philosophy and for some forms of imperialism that prevailed during the last few centuries. One of the basic principles of modern collectivism is the idea that the individual should sacrifice himself for the progress and welfare of the race. It is assumed that nature seeks to preserve the type: the pack, the herd or the hive and not the individual. Kaiser's as well as Hitler's Germany sought to apply this basis of collectivism within Germany and flaunt the idea of race superiority outside her borders.

But there cannot be any true culture unless we think of the individual, not as an egoistic unit but as a soul: and of society, not as a mere aggregation of human beings for certain economic, social, and political purposes, but as the larger soul of which the individual is a part. True unity can only spring out of a perception born of love. It will then be clear to us that the separate growth of the individual is as important as the equal and parallel development of society.

We may therefore say that science, which is master in the knowledge of processes and of apt machinery, cannot by itself contribute to the perfection of our being because it is ignorant of the foundation of our being and of world being.

Science has contributed a great deal to human welfare. Through the gospel of reason and experimental observation, by which it works, it has enabled man to acquire intellectual integrity and even purity of mind by cancelling vulgar and tawdry emotions. It has brought about a mechanized unity of material life. But it has also been responsible for ushering in a system of civilization which is too big for our limited mental capacity. It has multiplied our wants by creating new ones and it has facilitated aggressive domination by the collective ego. We have almost come to believe that the cult of the average man with his freedom and self-sufficiency and a perfected economy are the *summum bonum* of life.

If our passion for perfection is to be satisfied, we have to learn to communicate with the soul of the individual and not his ego. Psychology has to explore the higher mental planes

21

in order to be fully itself. Art has to probe further into the world of infinite beauty hidden in man's consciousness. Ethics has to discover that the law of good is nothing other than the law of God. The historian has not merely to study the mass movements and the economic and political events and vicissitudes that affect humanity. He has to discover in the panorama of events the underlying soul-pattern. The vital issue that faces man today is whether his progress has to be governed by the modern materialistic mind or by a nobler pragmatism, guided by spiritual culture and knowledge. An equilibrium has to be established between man's internal and external worlds. The following lines from Sri Aurobindo's *Vision of Science* state beautifully the crisis that confronts the modern man:

> *Thou hast forgot*
> *The Sphinx that waits for man beside the way*
> *All questions thou mayst answer but one day*
> *Her question shall await thee for reply,*
> *As all we must; for they who cannot, die*
> *She slays them and their mangled bodies lie*
> *Upon the highways of Eternity.*

4

Culture, Politics, and Religion

If culture, at its best, is concerned with the finer sense and sensitivity of man, politics is the aspect of human activity based on instincts, desires, and ambitions. Whatever the social, legal or ethical framework prescribed for him, the average politician fills it with a picture that reveals man in his lowest and most unenviable element. Political scientists of the behaviourist school believe that it is no use evaluating political activity in the light of norms and patterns of the higher life. They prefer to study realistically the patterns emerging from the regularly surging political activity around them.

India, since independence, has been passing through a momentous phase of developments in practically every field of national activity. New vistas are confronting us with hopes and challenges. A great democracy is forming itself for the first time on Indian soil and, despite manifold obstacles, is moving steadily towards its goal. An academic approach to our political life is sure to be of use in exploring life-giving and sustaining guidelines, extracting the general significance of day-to-day events and communicating it in a national perspective to an interested public. Such an approach itself is the product of an intensive study of the theory which has been formulated on the basis of earlier practice in various parts of the world.

It ensures dispassionate observation, inquiry and a genuine interest in the pattern implicitly present in the phenomena.

Speaking purely as a layman, innocent both of the profundities of political theory and the subtleties of political practice, I should like to say a word about one of the distinguishing features of political science which, in a way, is a science of the behaviour of coalitions. Some say that it is primarily concerned with action in the name of the state or government. Others think that the struggle for power inherent in every society is its distinctive feature. There is the third view that the pride of place should go to the realization of moral ideals. W.H. Riker, the author of *The Theory of Political Coalitions,* who holds that traditional methods—history writing, the description of institutions and legal analysis—have been exhausted, remarks that political science has yet to join economics and psychology in the creation of genuine sciences of human behaviour. For it has to rise above the level of wisdom literature by applying to political behaviour theories like the theory of games.

Riker's reference to "wisdom literature" seems to be full of ironic implications. He sounds like referring to nursery rhymes or fairy tales. But the realization of moral ideals need not be reduced to such a mockery. While it is certainly valuable to study the political behaviour of average human beings and discover the principles or patterns that underlie this phenomenon, it is equally desirable to study the political behaviour of people like Gandhiji, Sri Aurobindo, and Abraham Lincoln, to mention only a few. Their behaviour also is human, though it may be exceptional. Riker feels that a study of authoritative allocation of value is mostly reduced to the study of coalitions, for decisions are almost always taken by groups or subgroups which are coalitions, whether at the level of the individual, the party, or the nation. He adds that the general decision-making model is deeply biased towards the leader who wants nothing but power, the opportunistic leader, who uses ideology simply as a tool in building and winning coalitions. One may agree that the leader, who pays himself nothing of material value, has a bargaining advantage over the leader who tries to make some profit for himself. One who takes a cynical view of human nature is not surprised by the fact that the "typical leader of a coalition is the opportunistic leader". But there are other potentialities in human nature too. What about a leader like Gandhiji who wants neither material gain, nor power nor prestige, nor continuance in his role and yet can lead a coalition like the Congress of pre-independence days to a remarkable, if not a total, victory? Even the word "charisma" cannot explain the fact that idealism and a love of truth are responsible for the phenomenal success of such a leader. The charistimatic spell itself might be due to his idealism and love of truth. An analysis of leadership needs as much rightfully to to be presented in detail in a book on political science as an analysis of average human performance. One need not be a cynic in one's anxiety to be a realist. The idealist, on the other hand, need not recoil in horror from realism though it may be sordid. The political scientist has to take into account both idealism and realism as two facets of political behaviour and establish his thesis on this integral foundation.

One more instance may further clarify my point. Writing about the present balance of coalitions in world affairs, Riker says: "There stands no finer tribute to the essential modesty of the American character than the fact that, during the brief period of our exclusive possession of atomic weapons (i.e. 1945 onwards), the nation as a whole rejected as preposterous the temptation to establish world empire." The United States is a great country with a greatness that has a contemporary vitality. But I do not know how much of a tribute it would be

25

to the United States to say that the country did not make a bid for world domination.

Commenting further on what Riker calls the Age of Maneuvre in the present balance of coalitions in world politics, he points out that either through the prospect of systematic overpayment of allies by the United States and the Soviet Union or through mutual self-destruction, the two countries may be reduced to the state of dismembered followers and other more vigorous peoples may take up the leadership of the world. Either of the two countries must be the leader of a coalition comprising two-thirds of the world, if it is to dominate. Riker therefore suggests that the Age of Maneuvre could be prolonged indefinitely in the interest of world domination by the United States, the cost of leadership for the Soviet Union increased and that for the States reduced by allowing the Soviet alliance to grow to about a weight just greater than half. This theory may be welcome when applied to games. It may even be taken as being practised by the nations of the world today for each nation struggles to survive and dominate the world scene. But a war is different from a game of chess. It results, not in checkmating wooden pieces of various sizes and shapes but in destroying millions of human lives. Should we still be using the language of diplomacy in such contexts? Or should we, following Sri Aurobindo, whose birth centenary is to be celebrated in 1972, speak the language of seership, at he does in *The Ideal of World Unity:*

A division of the earth between the two systems, capitalistic and socialistic, seems for the present a more likely issue. In America the attachment to individualism and the capitalistic system of society and a strong antagonism not only to communism but to even a moderate socialism remains complete.... The extreme success of communism creeping

26

over the continents of the Old World . . . is yet, if we consider existing circumstances and the balance of opposing Powers, highly improbable and, even if it occurred, some accommodation would still be necessary.... A successful accommodation would demand the creation of a body in which all questions of possible dispute could be solved as they arose without any breaking out of open conflict, and this would be a successor of the League of Nations and the United Nations Organization and move in the same direction....This third body would be preserved by the same necessity or imperative utility of its continued existence.

It may be, as Hermann Heller says, that political science, dominated by the empirical and positivistic schools, and recently by the behaviouristic, "seeks on methodical grounds to avoid any idealistic formulations and to limit itself to a causal descriptive presentation of the political existent." But there are, as Heller himself admits, certain unchanging constants in the political process which elude the practical reason of the historicizing and sociologizing relativist. One of these constants is the nature of man as the product and at the same time the moulder of his history. But when human nature itself is an uncharted sea, the unchanging constant is also an unfathomed one. As Sri Aurobindo says in the opening paragraph of *The Ideal of Human Unity:*

The surfaces of life are easy to understand; their laws, characteristic movements, practical utilities are ready to our hand and we can seize on them and turn them to account with a sufficient facility and rapidity. But they do not carry us very far....Nothing is more obscure to humanity or less seized by its understanding, whether in the power that moves it or the sense of the aim towards which it moves,

27

than its own communal and collective life.

It may be worthwhile, therefore, in our application of theory to any political problem, to view it from an angle that integrates the two aspects of "politics" as a behavioural science and as a "policy science" or political philosophy. Like the United Nations Organization, political science should at least figure out the charter of human rights while confronting us with developments that are gross violations of the charter itself.

If some schools of political thought have no use for norms and patterns of human conduct, they can hardly be expected to influence political activity itself which is an unmitigated raw expression of human nature.

Some may hold science responsible for crimes that ought to be laid at the door of politicians. But scientists, like everybody else, are at the mercy of politicians. Politics has been described as the science of power. It is also the science of the utilization of power, whether it be horsepower, manpower, or atomic power. Scientists have helped establish mastery of man over his environment. The politician, however, has utilized science for forging destructive weapons. The politics of the split atom is far more dangerous than the power games of preceding ages. The atom is so small that two hundred million atoms, laid side by side, would total only one inch in length. A billion atoms cover only the head of a pin. An atomic blast can destroy the whole world. Atomic energy is, therefore, absolute power. Scientifically speaking, we live in the Atomic Age. Politically, we still belong to the Stone Age. The same old passion for domination and self-aggrandisement is ceaselessly at work in our midst. Our intellects have grown in Himalayan proportions but our hearts are still like unsplit atoms.

Providence seems to have determined to teach wisdom even if we are unwilling to learn it. Because atomic energy is absolute power, it can easily annihilate the human race. Nations will have to behave with other nations out of this fear of annihilation, if not through love. We therefore pay at least our lip homage to peace and hope, as President Eisenhower did, so that man's inventiveness shall not be "dedicated to his death, but consecrated to his life".

If culture is to prevail, atomic power has to be harnessed to uses beneficial to man. It may be used for increasing agricultural production by introducing radio-active tracers in fertilizers. It can bring about a revolution in food-handling methods. In the field of medicine, radio isotopes have been used for locating and curing brain tumours. Atomic power has made possible, in the field of industry, better textile and metal working plants. The shortage of coal and oil is said to be made up by atomic fuels. It is in this direction that knowledge and power have to be harnessed to the services of man in a cultured society. The politician has to stop brow-beating the scientist and exploiting him for mean ends.

The temple and the church are empty today, perhaps for good reasons. But the laboratories are full. More than the laboratories, it is the cinema theatres that are packed to capacity. This would be a great thing if the films that we produce observed the right values and did not exaggerate sex, or the struggle of one class against another, or the worship of the Goddess of Getting On. Science is benefactor, for any advancement of knowledge is bound to be beneficial. But there is a wolf in sheep's clothing that conceals itself behind science. This is the unashamed greed and selfishness of man, backed up by political power. We speak of one world, but how do we explain the extermination of American Indians, the destruction of Hiroshima, and the balance of power that foments continuous unrest in South-east Asia and in West Asia? If science has freed man from the horror of numerous diseases, it is now subjecting him to many more diseases hitherto unknown. Applied science has, in a large measure, banished as much joy from life as the human misery it has alleviated. It has turned man into a machine for making more machines. It takes an Aldous Huxley or a Charles Chaplin to depict the great harm that applied science has done to mankind. An invisible capitalist can now control the world market from his mansion or a Hitler or Stalin drive the world to rack and ruin from his office room. Science has brought about a directionless and rudderless world in which life becomes a nightmare and man a physical and mental wreck, a prey to unknown psychological diseases and a victim of hysteria and mass hypnosis. Applied science threatens to be a Frankenstein strangling its own creator.

An infinite longing to unravel the mystery of the world has been the basis of science. This has led to certain great results. But curiosity can also take an unhealthy turn when it is allied to evil or ignorance. It is human nature that has to change if science is to be put to better use.

Religion should not be confused with culture. A man of religion is not necessarily a man of culture. To be a religious man means to be a subscriber to a body of dogmas. In spite of his ethical behaviour and moral fervour, a man of religion may not be able to practise in his own life the formula for dynamic culture, the one that is based on a reconciliation of the spirit of one's times with the genius of all times. We have to think of religion, not as a body of dogmas, but as the science of the infinite. There is a logic and science of the infinite even as there is a logic and science of the finite.

This does not mean that we should rush to the other extreme and be victimized by one religion or the other. Religions have divided mankind. But religion in the singular, the spirit of religion or true spirituality, has always united human beings. Christianity may turn into churchanity and Hinduism degenerate into a number of polytheistic practices, but the essence of religion is love. The true spirit of religion has always said: "Listen to your conscience or inner voice, live in its light, even if the world goes against you". The true spirit of religion has always said, "be whole, you are three in one—a house divided against itself—a divided being whose word conflicts with deed, deed with thought and thought with feeling. You are a shattered person, integrate yourself." It also says, "Let service be your watchword. May love prevail. Let there be harmony between nation and nation."

Valmiki said: "Have respect for another's affection". Lord Krishna said: "Cling to Truth in the midst of all distractions". The Buddha counselled: "Have compassion for all living creatures". Christ advised: "Cultivate the innocence and purity of heart that children have". Unless science is guided and regulated by these majestic voices that have been heard through the ages, there can hardly be any hope for peace and delight in this world. Nor can there be any future for the diffusion of culture among the large masses of mankind.

AE, the Irish poet and mystic, has, in his book *The Interpreters*, posed the question: "When shall right find its appropriate might?" A character in the same book raises another question: "What relation have the politics of time with the politics of eternity?" These are questions which need to be pondered over, if we are really interested in finding a lasting solution to the crises of our age. Men of vision like Ashoka, Abraham Lincoln, and Gandhiji laid down their lives for reconciling the politics of time with the politics of eternity.

In *Savitri*, Sri Aurobindo presents a dialogue between the Goddess of Power at whose altar men worship and Savitri, the Soul. Savitri tells the Goddess:

Thou hast given men strength, wisdom thou couldst not give.

31

One day I will return, a bringer of light,
Then I will give to thee the mirror of God,
Thou shall see self and world as by him they are seen
Reflected in the bright pool of thy soul.
Thy wisdom shall be vast as thy power.
Then hate shall dwell no more in human hearts
And fear and weakness shall desert men's lives,
The cry of the ego shall be hushed within,
Its lion roar that claims the world as food,
All shall be might and bliss and happy force.

5

Culture of the East and the West

The question has been asked frequently: do the East and the West have distinctive cultural styles of their own? But are we sure of what we mean by "East" and "West"? The answer has been writ large over the pages of Dr Raghavan Iyer's book.[1] He points out that there has come to exist, during the last few centuries, "a distorting sense of distance, if not actually of alienation", between the two continents. It is, no doubt, true, as Wang Gungwu says, that "the cultures of the peoples of Asia are indeed heterogenous and cannot be lumped together even in contrast with European culture.... There is no single way of thinking generally applicable even to the East Asians."[2] But as he himself remarks, such concepts as "East Asia", "East", or the "Orient" were set up in opposition to the "Occident". He goes on to point out that the nations of East Asia, which, for long, cherished the desire to preserve and develop their respective cultures, adopted the slogan: "Asia is one" simply as a way of defending their respective cultures against the domination of the West.

There was some reason for this feeling too. Reincourt argued

[1]Raghavan Iyer (Ed.), *The Glass Curtain Between Asia and Europe*, OUP, 1965,
[2]*Ibid.*, p. 254,

that the ancient Asian cultures were to be viewed as those of terminated, arrested civilizations. Comte regarded Europe as the avant-garde of humanity. In his volume, *History the Betrayer,* R.H. Dance has exposed the European parochialism and prejudice in the teaching of history and the treatment of non-Christian religions. Indeed, a prejudice in the mind of the West against the East has been traced back to Herodotus, the father of European history. Dr Iyer's *Glass Curtain* shows, if anything, that the curtain is a real one and a cultured person has to be on his guard against it. It may be true, as Guenon and Coomaraswamy held, that there is no barrier between traditional cultures but only between the traditional East and the modern West. This need not obscure the relations between two parts of the world that had a common cultural heritage ranging from the days of the Eurasian hearth of civilization thousands of years ago. The modern West may feel now and then that Asia is a mere borrower and that she is only imitatting the intellectual and technical achievements of Europe. This wrong historical perspective has to be set right. To quote Joseph Needham:

> To suppose that pure and applied science sprang fully formed from the body of the European Renaissance is entirely false; there had been a long preparation of centuries which had seen the absorption by all Europe of Arabic learning, Indian thought, and Chinese technology. The physico-mathematical hypotheses of Galileo can hardly be visualised without Indian numeral notation. The arsenal in which he set the scene of one of his world-changing dialogues could not have accomplished much without mastery of the characteristic Chinese technique of iron-casting.[3]

[3]*Ibid.,* p. 283.

34

Knowledge is not the private property of any nation or continent. It always belongs to the world community. The Asian heritage needs to be presented in detail to the world today to bring all parts of the world closer.

This mode of thinking also is as old as Herodotus. In fact, Herodotus ridiculed the notion that any portion of mankind was one-eyed and distinct from the rest. He wondered why three different names—derived from the names of women—had been given to the earth which is but one. As Gandhiji also said: "The only lesson to be learnt is that the East and West are no more than names. Human beings are the same everywhere. He who wants to will conduct himself with decency. There is no people for whom the moral life is a special mission. Everything depends on the individual himself."

The Glass Curtain, therefore, can clearly be transcended. Here is Geoffrey Hudson's eloquent exposition of this prospect from the same book:

... the new generalised cosmopolitan culture of this age has at last put us at a new point of vantage for apprehension of all the great cultural systems of the past, since all these, including our own, have lost their exclusive hold, while the whole cultural heritage of humanity, of whatever civilisation, is more available and accessible to the ordinary educated man, if he wishes to explore it, then it has ever been before. The arrogant cultural self-sufficiency of the 19th century Europe, judging Eastern philosophy, literature and arts by its own standards and conventions, is giving place, under conditions in which there is no longer any European world supremacy, to a much greater freedom of approach to all cultural phenomena, a more comprehensive and eclectic taste. In spite of the current excesses of political nationalism, a genuine citizenship of the world has become more of a practical possibility in the cultural sphere than at any time in the past history of man.[4]

It may be rather facile to think with Lowes Dickinson that the psychological barrier between the East and the West will disappear with the inevitable "Westernization" of the East. There is Jaspers on the other side warning us that Europe today is a burnt-out volcano and that there is a danger of Europe "sinking" back into Asia. For all we know, there may also be a distinctive Asian mode of modernization.

W.B. Yeats looked forward to the begetting by Asia on Europe of a new spiritual era in the West.

Without committing ourselves to any of these statements, it is still possible to maintain that Europe and Asia have through the ages evolved cultural styles of their own, though both these styles reveal only minor variations within the general pattern of world culture that we have in view. We may discuss the implications of this statement, particularly with reference to India and the West.

There is a beautiful myth in the *Padma Purana,* which is also presented with some variations in a few other Sanskrit classics. It is the story of the churning of the ocean by gods and demons. Ranged on either side but for a common quest—the discovery of the nectar of immortality—they used the *Mandara* mountain as their churning rod and *Vasuki,* the great python, as the rope with which to turn the rod. As a result of this churning, the sea yielded successively to them *kaustubha,* the invaluable jewel which Vishnu later wore, the *parijata* tree, *uchhaisravas,* the winged horse, *airavata,* the white elephant which came to be used as his favourite transport animal by Indra, god of heaven, the moon who, in Indian mythology, is said to be the

[4]*Ibid.,* p. 323.

offspring of the mind and Lakshmi, the gooddess of beauty and fine arts, crudely linked by merchants with wealth and commercial success.

So far, so good. But at this point in the story, the further churning of the ocean throws up *apsaras* or the sirens. At that very moment, *Vasuki* reaches down its mouth to the rocky bottom of the sea and bites a piece of stone. By this act of the python poison is generated and it spreads like fire all over the world and begins to consume it. In order to save creation from this calamity, Shiva drinks all that poison but retains it in the throat, thus becoming the blue-throated god. The gods and demons continue to churn the ocean and then is nectar born. A fierce struggle ensues between the gods and demons for the exclusive possession of this elixir of life. It is at this point in the story that Vishnu appears on the scene as *mohini*, an enchantress, and cleverly manages to see that the gods have all the nectar to themselves, thus becoming immortal. The demons' ambition to achieve immortality is foiled.

The gods and demons in this myth are not just figures from nowhere. They symbolize the forces of good and evil that are operating ceaselessly in human society. The ocean itself is a symbol of life lived under the dominion of time and eternity. The Mandara mountain, the churning rod, stands for the energy, intelligence, and imagination expended by man on the great task of mastering the strange and inexplicable universe in which he is called upon to live. The python symbolizes his will and his desire for mastery of various kinds.

What follows, step by step, is the story of human evolution. Man becomes lord of metals, passing through the Stone, the Bronze and the Iron Ages. He takes the *kaustubha* to his bosom and gradually extends his dominion over the world of plants, animals, the realm of his own mind and of the fine arts, having discovered the charm of introspection (the moon) and the contemplation and communication of Beauty (Lakshmi). Human civilization reaches its acme of glory, its peak of excellence at this point.

But more than energy, will, intelligence, and imagination is needed to retain what is won and march ahead. Man loses his stability and balance when temptations beset him and sirens call out to him from the islands of enchantment. Many ancient civilizations, ancient Indian civilization itself, split on this rock of man's incapacity for self-conquest. This is also the problem :hat both Europe and America face today. With all their gigantic ordering of resources, they have created a bewildering social structure amidst which the individual lives an alienated life and faces temptations continually, succumbing to them at one time or the other. This is how the python bites a piece of rock at the bottom of the sea and poison from the streams of life spreads all around.

Spirituality was the dominant motive of Indian civilization. But during her Dark and Middle Ages, the synthesis that she had achieved of matter and spirit, of reason and intuition, the reconciliation of the individual and the collective broke down. Spirituality, the dominant motive of her civilization, became anaemic, unsupported by economic self-sufficiency, science, and the spirit of free enquiry. Bent on the exclusive quest for the nectar of immortality and strangely unmindful of the prime need for the *kaustubha,* the *parijata*, the *uchhaisravas,* and *airavata,* the moon and Mahalakshmi for an integral life, she plunged into an ocean, not of delight, but of sorrow.

There are two principles governing the cultural life—the principle of matter and the principle of spirit, the principle of time and the principle of eternity. Any individual or organization that wishes to evolve culturally has to remain loyal to both these principles. Otherwise, there will be imbalance and instability. If Europe has been too much a creature of the Time

Spirit, India has been the victim of the Absolute.

Indian society stagnated at a particular stage of its growth by giving primacy to the spiritual salvation of the individual, excluding all responsibility for collective living. The Buddha insisted that he would live in the earth atmosphere till the last human being was spiritually emancipated. But it was difficult for every individual to cultivate Buddha's ideal of life. It was too rigorous a discipline for the average man.

The distinction that Aristotle made between private and public virtues is very useful in this context. The Renaissance ideal of magnificence aims at cultivating all the twelve virtues, public and private, for the perfection of the individual. At some stage in India, public virtues tended to be ignored. The cultured man thought, as a rule, of his own personal salvation or of the spiritual salvation of the people around him. He rarely bent his energies to the task of freedom and governance of his country, the betterment of living conditions for his people, and the conquest of new knowledge for harnessing it to the cause of their material well-being. All that had to wait till the Indian Renaissance set in motion a fresh current of ideas.

Sri Aurobindo has brought this out beautifully in *The Foundations of Indian Culture*. The representative Indian attitude, as expressed in the Vedas and Upanishads, was not one of an anaemic spirituality. This happened in certain contexts which we may discuss later. Spirituality, in its representative Indian form, embraced all life, from its innermost core to its outermost rind or shell. It penetrated time as well as eternity, finitude and infinity. "The Indian," says Sri Aurobindo, "believes that the ultimate truths are truths of the spirit and that truths of the spirit are the most fundamental and most effective truths of our existence, powerfully creative of the inner, salutarily reformative of the outer life. To the European the ultimate truths are more often truths of the ideative intellect, the pure reason."[5] The only verifying "tests of values" come from the ordinary action of the mind, life and body and the rest are speculations, their proper place "is in the world of ideas, not of life".

Comparing the peak points of European with those of Indian civilization Sri Aurobindo remarks:

Two things especially distinguish the normal European mind —for we must leave aside some great souls and some great thinkers or some moments or epochs of abnormal religiosity and look at the dominant strain. Its two significant characters are the cult of the inquiring, defining, effective, practical reason and the cult of life. The great high tides of European civilization, Greek culture, the Roman world before Constantine, the Renaissance, the modern age with its two colossal idols, industrialism and physical science, have come to the West on the strong ascending urge of this double force. Whenever the tide of these powers has ebbed, the European mind has entered into much confusion, darkness and weakness. Christianity failed to spiritualize Europe, whatever it may have done towards humanizing it in certain ethical directions because it ran counter to these two master instincts; it denied the supremacy of the reason and put its anathema on a satisfied or strenuous fullness of life. But in Asia there has been neither this predominance of the reason or the life-cult nor any incompatability of these two powers with the religious spirit. The great ages of Asia, the strong culminations of her civilization and culture in India —the high Vedic beginning, the grand spiritual stir of the Upanishads, the wide flood of Buddhism, Vedanta, Sankhya,

[5]Sri Aurobindo, *The Foundation of Indian Culture*, p. 6.

the Puranic and Tantric religions, the flowerings of Vaishna-
vaism and Shaivism in the Southern kingdoms—have come
in on a surge of spiritual light....It was in such periods
that intellect, thought, poetry, the arts, the material life
flowed into splendour. The ebbing of spirituality brought
in always on the contrary, the weakness of these other
powers, periods of fossilization or at least depression of the
power of life, tracts of decline, even beginnings of decay.
This is a clue to which we have to hold if we would understand the great lines of divergence between the East and
the West.[6]

Indian culture began to decline when it came increasingly to
be associated with a regular withdrawal from life. In this connection the image of India plunged into an ocean of sorrow
because of her exclusive preoccupation with spirit, separated
from the other powers and godheads of life. Again, Sri
Aurobindo has described this process of disintegration beautifully:

India's internal and individual seeking of the spirit and
ideals of our civilization was vigorous. But the application
in the collective life of society was subjected to serious
reserves. Never bold and thorough-going, it became more
and more limited and halting when the life-force declined
in her peoples. This defeat, this gulf between ideal and
collective practice, has pursued all human living and was
not peculiar to India; but the dissonance became especially
marked with the lapse of time and it put at last on our
society a growing stamp of weakness and failure. There was
a large effort in the beginning at some kind of synthesis

[6]*Ibid.,* pp. 85-6.

between the inner ideal and the outer life; but a static regulation of society was its latter end. An underlying principle of spiritual idealism, an elusive unity and fixed helpful forms of mutuality remained always there, also an increasing element of strict bondage and minute division and fissiparous complexity in the social mass. The great Vedantic ideals of freedom, unity and the godhead in man were left to the inner spiritual effort of individuals. The power of expansion and assimilation diminished and when powerful and aggressive forces broke in from outside, Islam, Europe, the later Hindu society was content with an imprisoned and static self-preservation, a mere permission to live. The form of living became more and more narrow and it endured a continually restricted assertion of its ancient spirit. Duration, survival was achieved, but not in the end a really secure and vital duration, not a great robust and victorious survival.[7]

It is not for nothing that I have quoted these paragraphs at length. Sri Aurobindo lays his finger unerringly on the fundamental distinction between the civilizations of India and Europe and supports his point by referring to their illustrative peak periods of excellence. He gives an unsparing analysis of the decline of Indian civilization, pointing out how, when the life-force declined, the application of the ideal in the collective life of society also declined, resulting only in survival, but not a robust and victorious survival. A whole history of the evolution and decline of Indian culture, tracing it step by step in the manner set forth by Sri Aurobindo in the paragraph quoted above, waits to be written by a seasoned scholar.

There are two important points in this connection. The

[7]*Ibid.*, p. 38.

"spirituality" of India is usually contrasted with the "materialism" of the West. In this context, "spirituality" connotes an otherworldiness of disposition, an indifference to the ordering of the collective life of society, and an exclusive and almost anaemic preoccupation with spirit divorced from other manifestations of reality, obsessed with personal salvation. For Sri Aurobindo, the word "spirituality" has a totally different meaning. It is the blossom and fruit of life, the green of its leaves, the very expression in the countenance of all life. His concept of "spirituality" is robustly full-blooded and embraces all activity. The fall of a leaf on the grass is an act permeated as much by spirit as the sublime vision of the cosmic spirit that Arjun had in the battlefield. The mundane is penetrated and permeated and has to be transformed by spirit. Indian civilization began with such a permeation and transfusion and what it strived to achieve was a transformation of this kind in the individual and collective life. It failed all the more. What survived was only a sense of this transfusion and permeation.

Sri Aurobindo had also a crystal clear vision of the lines on which Indian civilization is going to develop in the coming years. It is not as though Indian civilization withered away and another civilization is springing up in its place. After the ancient phase, Indian civilization met with various challenges, Islam and the West being the two major challenges. It then set out to assimilate them in its own way, becoming more and more composite in the process.

Sri Aurobindo also suggests the way out:

And now survival itself has become impossible without expansion. If we are to live at all, we must resume India's great interrupted endeavour; we must take up boldly and execute thoroughly in the individual and in the society, in the spiritual and in the mundane life, in philosophy and religion, in art and literature, in thought, in political and economic and social formulation the full and unlimited sense of her highest spirit and knowledge. And if we do that, we shall find that the best of what comes to us, draped in occidental forms, is already implied in our own ancient wisdom and has a greater spirit behind it, a profounder truth, self-knowledge and the capacity of a will to nobler and more ideal formulations. Only we need to work out throughly in life what we have always known in the spirit. There and nowhere else lies the secret of the needed harmony between the essential meaning of our past culture and the environmental requirements of our future.[8]

Our doctrine of secularism has to be reviewed and examined in this context. Secularism should not stand for a mere negation of religion. There is no objection to each religion being practised by those who profess it. Since each religion has in it something imperishable and universal and also some features of the social, political, and cultural organization of the time when it was founded, the individuals professing each religion —their leaders or prophets—may like to modernize the social, political, and cultural features, retaining intact what is imperishable and universal. This would be a movement for religious reform. Secularism comes in, mainly as a basis or meeting-ground for persons who profess different faiths in an atmosphere of mutual understanding, tolerance and goodwill for the consideration or execution of those plans and regulations which affect them all in the collective life of the nation. But Sri Aurobindo does not stop here. He observes that the characteristic achievement of India as a nation and her contribution to world culture lies in the resumption of India's "great

[8]*Ibid.,* pp. 38-9.

interrupted endeavour", that of executing "in the individual and in society, in the spiritual and in the mundane life, in art and literature, in thought, in political and economic and social formulation the full and unlimited sense of her highest spirit and knowledge." This is the genius of India as a nation and this will fulfill itself when her children, whatever the religion they profess, each group through the images and symbols that it elects to employ, meet in a secular atmosphere and set themselves the task of transfusing the light of spirit into all departments of human activitity and transforming them in that light.

Speaking of culture from a global point of view, the unique gift of India to mankind has been the formulation of a process of psychological evolution possible to man and divested of all dogma, which takes him from the circumference of his personality to its very centre, enables him to arrive at an utter identity with the world and God, the microcosm with the macrocosm, and makes him the heir of all the ages and the pilgrim of eternity. This is not all. All the paths that lead him to this glory—self-control, works, wisdom, devotion, contemplation—have been traced and set forth in the fullest detail so that the individual may choose the path of his preference to reach the summit of his own personality. What is more, the cultural history of India, from the hoary past to the present century, has been star-strewn with shining examples of this formulation and path-finding, this aspiration and fulfilment.

The West could not have given this gift to mankind. But it has had something else to give in modern times, almost equally precious—discovery, or the continuous unravelling of the mystery of nature, invention or the steady extension of the dominion of man over his environment and exploration or the conquest of subterranean and interstellar space. Almost equally precious, for, without this knowledge, man would be a caveman in an unfamiliar world. If the gifts that the West

45

gives are the gifts of time, India's gift is the gift of eternity.

The question has often been asked whether European civilization is disintegrating today. Kroeber, the celebrated anthropologist who attempts an answer to this question, says that the existing aesthetic style patterns of European civilization have been definitely attacked and disrupted from 1910 onwards. The two world wars have created tensions in most aspects of the civilization. But at the same time, population, wealth, communication, industry, and science have still been expanding vigorously and European culture is spreading rapidly to the "empty" areas of America, Australia, Asia, and Africa and is tending to supplant native cultures and transform old native civilizations in Asia and Africa. The Russian way of life Kroeber looks upon only as a competing variant within the European civilization itself. The successful culture of contemporary Russia, he thinks, emanates from Western civilization and is increasingly assimilating to it. The United States, British-derived in history, speech and culture, is the counterpoise to Russia in resources and strength. The only shift that Kroeber sees is that of the centre of power and wealth productivity from Western-central Europe to the peripheral East and West. He recognizes indications that the peripheral East and West may come to dominate in creativity too.

Kroeber argues on this basis that it is still uncertain whether this interval will prove to be a reconstruction to a new phase within Western civilization or lead to a basically new and distinct civilization. He thinks that the latter alternative seems somewhat the less likely because of the growth which continues successfully in so many segments of the existing Western culture—in contrast to the inter-classic-Western interval of the Dark Ages, which was almost wholly retractile or disintegrative.[9]

This falls in line with what I have said regarding Eastern and Western culture from a global point of view. If European civilization is tending to transform old native civilizations in Asia and Africa, the old native civilization of Asia, as W.B. Yeats foresaw, is tending to beget on Europe a new spiritual era in the West. This is how a global culture may come into its own, gathering together the best that has been felt, thought and done in different parts of the world.

[9]A.L. Kroeber, *A Roster of Civilization and Culture,* Aldine Publishing Company, Chicago, USA, 1962, p. 29.

6

Ancient Indian Culture

Ancient Indian culture has been loved and hated, admired and ridiculed, but rarely understood in its totality, subtlety, and full-bloodedness. The scholar and the common man have taken from it what they have fancied. If some are in love with Vatsyayana's *Kamasutras* and the illustrations of these aphorisms carved in those epics of stone, the temples of India, others are in raptures over its poetry or grammar, its science of cookery or metaphysics. Ancient Indian culture has meant many things to many people but rarely the same luminous totality to most of them.

The reason for this tragedy or comedy of errors is the fact that many of its interpreters have looked at it only with a partial vision, pressing it into service for riding their own hobby horses. The currency of the words *maya* and *nirvana* in Europe makes it obvious that the average European views ancient Indian culture as a cult of self-denial, unworldly in its aim and negative in its vision. To those who are unable to see the wood for the trees, the temple shrine for the sculpured panels, and the God of the Hindu imagination for its prolife-rating gods and goddesses, ancient Indian culture has meant paganism run riot. To those who are unable to perceive the significance of daring symbols, it has seemed to be a strange amalgam of sex and spirituality. One has to remember the sixty four *vidyas* orl ores that had to be acquired, if one was to be called a cultured or accomplished person. It is only then that one perceives that the ancient Indian concept of culture was far more magnificent and comprehensive than the concept of the European Renaissance—that of the all-inclusive virtue of magnificence such as was embodied in a hero like King Arthur. It stood for the cultivation of life in all its infinite variety and totality. It measured the heights, depths, and the vast expanses of life, encompassing earth and heaven. It was the whole man that ancient Indian culture had in view, not merely economic, hedonistic, social or spiritual man. Its wholeness of vision has hardly been equalled. The culture of Greece and Rome left out some of the most valuable components included in the Indian system. European civilization suffers from a strong one-sidedness and its achievements are spectacularly lop-sided. The Indian scholar, till recently, was inclined to speak of the metaphysical grandeur of Indian culture. Sri Aurobindo was amongst the first to see that, from the Vedas, which were no mere primitive hymns addressed to anthropomorphic deities, right down to Vidyaranya, what fascinated the Indian mind was the life-play from its simplest to its most profound implications.

The pre-history of ancient Indian culture, receding beyond the Harappa and Vedic Ages, is linked up with the pre-history of several other ancient cultures. Kroeber, in his essay on the ancient Oikoumene as a historic culture aggregate, has made certain interesting remarks on ancient Indian civilization as a whole. "Oikoumene" means the "inhabited". The Greeks referred this to the total habitable world known in their time. It stretched from the Pillars of Hercules to the Indian Ocean and the Seres. The tracts referred to by the Greeks still correspond to a great historic unit. It was within this frame that the most important forms of civilization, as yet produced by mankind, were achieved. The tracts cover the eastern end of the Mediterranean from Egypt to Mesopotamia, Greece and Rome, Persia, India, China, Champa, Cambodia, Siam and Java, France, and northern Europe. Eastward, was the Fertile Crescent, Persia, China, colonial India and Japan. Westward, was the Fertile Crescent again, Crete, Greece, Rome and the Atlantic Europe. There was continous interaction among those areas. It has only recently begun to be known to what extent Greek science rested on antecedents in the Fertile Crescent. The Greek sculpture had its impact on the Gandhara sculpture. The way the art of papermaking travelled all the way from China to Europe is well known. Kroeber says that the Oikoumene was the region of the first hearth of all higher civilizations, of the first farming, towns, and kings and letters.

Islam arose in this region at a time when constructive cultural impulses had long since moved out of that hearth and even beyond Greece and Persia. The region lay covered by a presumably uncongenial Hellenic and Persian civilization. The societies of Egypt, Syria, and Mesopotamia were also worn out. Kroeber finds significance in the fact that Islam arose in this very region to establish an individual free society. Islamic civilization was new precisely in its appeal to the common techniques and therefore to the commonness of men and in its discarding of much of the past heritage. It reduced and simplified culture.

Indian culture emerged in the same mundane way in which other cultures of the Eurasian hearth arose and shared the same cultural materials across the breadth of the Oikoumene. It had the same basic subsistence and survival techniques like the growing of food crops such as wheat, the breeding of cattle and other animals, and the cultivation of metallurgical processes. It believed in the divinity of kingship and in eunuchism.

It shared the same systems of magico-ritual practice like astrology and alchemy and divination from parts of animals. The taming of horses, the use of chariots and the stirrup saddle, disk coinage, water-mills, the use of cotton—all these features spread from one end of the area to the other emerging from some part of it, like the use of cotton from India. The use of seals, compass, game of chess which originated in India, falconry, the use of the crossbow, and the concept of the dragon were also items shared in common by these cultures. The display of wealth in royal burials, sculptures, drama—these were the other common features. Thus as Kroeber, who writes about the Oikoumene, says, within this great web of cultural growth, inventions or new cultural materials tended to be transmitted from end to end, though the major style of each civilization in the area persisted in its individuation. Later, new ways of thinking also showed a tendency to propagate themselves across this area like a wave. The common stock from which Indian civilization arose awaits, as yet, the Indian scholar who will make its study in depth.

The Harappan and Vedic phases of Indian civilization are yet imperfectly known. The Vedic period is said to extend from about B.C. 2000 to B.C. 600. What exactly transpired between the Harappans and the Aryans that came over and settled down in India is capable of varying interpretations. That there was a commingling of Harappan and Vedic cultures is certain, though precise details of this commingling are not yet beyond controversy. Several Vedic hymns might possibly have been composed and been current among the Aryan groups that came to India, even before they came. Some of the hymns might have been simple utterances connected with ritual or anthropomorphism such as one usually associates with primitive people. But scholastic Indian priests, European and Indian scholars trained in their tradition have, I believe,

51

done a great injustice to the metaphysical implications contained in the hymns of the *Rig Veda*. It is a matter of regret that the original contribution made by Sri Aurobindo in this field in *The Secret of the Veda* is hardly noticed even now in our university departments of Sanskrit or ancient Indian culture. I have discussed the philological basis for Sri Aurobindo's interpretation of *The Rig Veda* in my book, *The Poetic Approach to Language.* This is what Sri Aurobindo says about the subject:

> The Veda became to the later scholastic and ritualistic idea of Indian priests and pundits nothing better than a book of mythology and sacrificial ceremonies; European scholars seeking in it what was alone to them of any rational interest, the history, myths and popular religious notions of a primitive people, have done yet worse wrong to the Veda and by insisting on a wholly external rendering still farther stripped it of its spiritual interest and its poetic greatness and beauty.

The poets of the Vedic verse were not just silly shepherds, herdsmen and medicine-men to a robust and barbarous tribe. They were seers and thinkers, *rsi, dhira.* "These singers," says Sri Aurobindo, "believed that they were in possession of a high, mystic and hidden truth, claimed to be the bearers of a speech acceptable to a divine knowledge, and expressly so speak of their utterances, as secret words which declare their whole significance only to the seer, *Kavaye nivacanani ninya vacamsi.* And to those who came after them the Veda was a book of knowledge, and even of the supreme knowledge, a revelation."[2]

What are these "secret words" which reveal their significance

[1]Sri Aurobindo, *The Foundation of Indian Culture,* 1959, p. 74.
[2]*Ibid.,* p. 275.

only to the seer? As said earlier, I have discussed this question at some length elsewhere. I need only mention here the fact that, in "ancient" languages, words are multi-semantic. They have whole or undivided meanings. This is seen, for example, in a Latin word like *spiritus* which means "wind, breath, spirit". Poets could use words of this kind with one of their meanings in the forefornt of their minds, the others being in the background. Only the initiated would know the mystical or psychological meaning. Language was used in this "secret" way, by taking advantage of the multi-semanticism of words, in order to keep the expression of subtle and mystical experiences away from the uninitiated. Ancient symbols and myths have undivided meanings and this explains their enduring freshness and charm. Owen Barfield thinks that when poets use metaphors in poetry, they are trying to restore old undivided meanings to words. Thus when in Shakespeare's *Antony and Cleopatra,* a character refers to Antony as: "The noble *ruin* of her magic, Antony", the Latin sense of the word *ruin* as "fall" ("Heaven *ruining* from Heaven": Milton's *Paradise Lost*) is retained, for the word refers to Antony's fall from his exalted position and the loss of empire, all because of his infatuation. But the word also hints at Antony's moral ruin, his dereliction of duty and of Octavia, his wife, though he is a "noble ruin".

But words were themselves mult-semantic in ancient-languages and the Vedic poets could employ them consistently for conveying various levels of meaning. They used this power of primitive words in a special way. Sri Aurobindo says:

An outward figure nearest to the inward experience, its material counterpart, is taken and used with such realism and consistency that while it indicates to those who possess it the spiritual experience, it means only the external thing

53

to others. . . . The physical and the psychical words were to their eyes a manifestation and a twofold and diverse and yet connected and similar figure of cosmic godheads, and behind was the one spirit of Being of which the Gods were names and personalities and powers. . . . The life of man was to these seers a thing of mixed truth and falsehood, a movement from mortality to immortality... a battle between the children of Light and the sons of Night, a getting of treasure, of the wealth, the booty given by the gods to the human warrior, and a journey and a sacrifice; and of these things they spoke in a fixed system of images taken from Nature and from the surrounding life of the warlike, pastoral and agricultural Aryan peoples and centred round the cult of Fire and the worship of the powers of living Nature and the institution of sacrifice. The details of outward existence and of the sacrifice were in their life and practice symbols, and in their poetry not dead symbols or artificial metaphors, but living and powerful suggestions and counterparts of inner things. . . . It is evident that a poetry of this kind, written by men with this kind of vision or imagination, cannot either be interpreted or judged by the standards of a reason and taste observant only of the canons of the physical existence. The invocation "Play, Ray, and become towards us" is at once a suggestion of the leaping up and radiant play of the potent sacrificial flame on the physical altar and of a similar psychical phenomenon, the manifestation of the saving flame of a divine power and light within us. The western critic sneers at the bold and reckless and to him monstrous image in which Indra, son of earth and heaven is said to create his own father and mother; but if we remember that Indra is the supreme spirit in one of its eternal and constant aspects, creator of earth and heaven, born as a cosmic godhead between the mental and physical

world and recreating their powers in man, we shall see that
the image is not only a powerful but in fact a true and
revealing figure, and in the Vedic technique it does not
matter that it outrages the physical imagination since it
expresses a greater actuality as no other figure could have
done with the same awakening aptness and vivid poetical
force. The Bull and Cow of the Veda, the shining herds of
the Sun, lying hidden in the cave, are strange enough creatures
to the physical mind, but they do not belong to the earth
and in their own plane they are at once images and actual
things and full of life and significance.[3]

Thus *agni* in the Veda is fire as well as the psychic fire within
us. The *gous* or cows are kine as well as rays of divine light.
Indra is the flaming warrior god as well as the Divine Will. To
misinterpret this sublime mystical poetry as crude and primitive anthropomorphism is to misunderstand the core of Indian
culture, its very essence. One only hopes that the departments
of ancient Indian culture will promote a study of the Veda on
these lines.

The terminal phase of ancient Indian culture has been the
subject-matter of controversy. Where exactly did the ancient
Indian phase end and the medieval phase begin? The Bhavan
history of India adopts the following chronological divisions:

1. *The Vedic Age:* from the earliest times to B.C. 600.
2. *The Age of Imperial Unity brought about by the Mauryas:*
   B.C. 600 to 320 A.D.
3. *The Classical Age:* 320 to 750 A.D.
4. *The Age of Imperial Kanauj:* 750 to 1000 A.D.
5. *The Struggle for Empire:* 1000 to 1300 A.D.

[3]*Ibid.,* pp. 279-81.

This nomenclature is somewhat inadequate with reference to the fourth and fifth items. It does no justice to the great political and cultural movements in the South. The ancient Indian phase is said to end by the year 1300 A.D. Another view is that the medieval phase begins with the accession of Qutb-ud-Din to the throne of Delhi in 1206 A.D. A third school holds that there is a marked decadence in all cultural activity about 1000 A.D. onwards and that the period from 1000 A.D. to 1300 A.D. should be regarded as a long period of struggle for political supremacy. Whatever the solution acceptable to the majority of historians, the important thing to do is to have a time and space-profile of the distinctive features of ancient Indian civilization that continued to be active in various parts of India beyond the dividing line—wherever it happens to be drawn—between the ancient and medival phases. For example, the Vijayanagara Empire was founded in the South in 1336 A. D., beyond the dividing line. Ancient Indian civilization continued to be active there and one could even speak of glorious achievements in many spheres of cultural activity. The Marathas took it up when Vijayanagara fell. Some of the Rajput states had similar achievements to their credit. In a few princely States, like Mysore and Baroda, some features of ancient Indian culture held their habitual sway even in the 19th century and life went on undisturbed in minor princely States. What were the customs and traditions of ancient Indian civilization that were retained and projected in this way even during the medieval phase? What is their time-and-space profile? Scholars have yet to examine these problems and organize research projects in these areas.

There was, no doubt, resistance offered by the ancient culture to the alien culture and to the more composite one that was growing up during the Middle Ages. But the Middle Ages have to be regarded as a period of reconstitution as much as of resistance. The ancient pattern was retained and even revived wherever resistance was strong. The resistance itself absorbed some of the features of the alien culture.

We shall also have to examine those features of the civilization that have been integrated into the medieval phase. The retention and continuation of these features is one thing and their combination with emergent features to form new cultural items and styles, whether at the subsistence, social or "value" level, quite another. This means we shall first have to form a clear idea of what medieval Indian civilization stands for. Saints like Nanak and Kabir and emperors like Akbar had certain relevant things to say on the value aspect. The lives and utterances of leaders of thought and action who flourished during the medieval phase will have to be studied from this point of view.

This also holds good with reference to the modern period and, probably, with greater force. The Indian Renaissance had many spokesmen who examined all aspects of cultural activity and spoke clearly and boldly about them. Several ancient cultural values have entered into the modern Indian concept of culture and stayed there for more than a century. The cultural debate of the twentieth century in India centres around the acceptance or rejection of some features of the ancient Indian value system and also around the other issue: which of the values of contemporary Western civilization shall we accept? The entire body of pronouncements on Indian culture from Ram Mohun Roy to Vinoba Bhave will have to be reviewed in order to ascertain what features of the ancient and medieval pattern persist in the structure of the emergent value-system and how much of Western civilization it has absorbed.

While taking the successive phases of ancient Indian civilization into account, we shall have to reckon with the intensity and climax of this civilization, its peak-points of excellence.

For example, there is the phenomenon of the clustering of great minds at a particular moment in a country's history. The Upanishadic sages probably represent such a great moment. It is interesting to know that the Buddha, Mahavira, and Panini were contemporaries in the 6th century B.C. There was another outburst of glory during the age of Kalidasa, under the Guptas. There is, as Kroeber says: "A correlation between realized genius and opportunity given by a stage of civilization's development—the stage when its productive cultural patterns are defined and mature but where their inherent potentialities have not yet begun to be exhausted."[4] He further remarks: "What we were wont to call 'great men' are those among many more individuals of above average ability who happen to get born in a time and place and society, the patterns of whose culture have formed with sufficient potential value and have developed to sufficient ripeness to allow the full capacities of these individuals to be realized or expressed."

The study of the consanguinity of talent—of the activity of select groups or the direction of cultural or literary movements—has yet to be taken up so as to make these great historical moments in ancient Indian culture understandable to the common man. This has been done with admirable thoroughness for European literature. The achievements of cultural or literary groups like the German Romantics or the French symbolists have been made part of the cherished possession of an average student of European literature—through such a presentation. If English literature is to be taken to illustrate the point, which lover of English literature in India does not know the pre-Shakespearian university wits, the Mermaid Tavern, the metaphysicals, Dr Johnson and his circle, the Romantics and the Pre-Raphaelites? It may be that for

[4]Kroeber, *The Nature of Culture,* p. 128.

Sanskrit and Prakrit literatures, there is the difficulty of chronology, Indian history being elusive material. But this difficulty persists about the world-renowned Shakespeare himself, though he was born only about four hundred years ago. There are students of Shakespeare's plays even today who seriously maintain that Shakespeare was not the author of those plays. It will, no doubt, be possible to identify outstanding moments or groups in the history of Sanskrit or Praktit literatures, a coherent and intimate account of which will give the common man an illuminating idea of his cultural heritage.

Another interesting question we have to ask ourselves is about the unity and continuity of Indian culture. Did it really disintegrate or did it start reconstituting itself during its medieval and modern phases? In a lyrical and beautiful paragraph in his Preface to *The Vedic Age* (Vol. I), Dr R.C. Majumdar remarks:

This volume attempts a picture of what may be regarded as the dawn of Hindu civilization. To continue the metaphor, we may say that the next two volumes reflect its full morning glory and noonday splendour; in the fourth volume we come across the shadows of the declining day, while dusk sets in with the fifth. Then follows the darkness of the long night, so far as Hindu civilization is concerned, a darkness which envelops it even now.

Dr Majumdar shows that it is possible to look at this phenomenon from another angle. "One may rightly question," he says, "the reasonableness of designating historical periods by the religious denomination of the ruling dynasties.... We have accordingly divided Indian history into three chronological periods—ancient, medieval and modern."

Let us examine this question a little more closely. Ancient

Indian civilization, which was Hindu, had itself a composite origin. The Dravadian and the Aryan, not to mention other races, contributed considerably to its evolution. It was further developed by a people who professed not one, but at least three different faiths, not to mention other minor creeds. One of the three faiths—Vedic, Jain, and Buddhist—prevailed over the other two during one or the other of the ancient phases in some part of India or the other, looking at it from the point of view of the religious denomination of the ruling dynasties. A profound change ensued later in the cultural pattern of India, for more diverse races and faiths came in—the Turks, Afghans, Moghuls, Islam, and Christianity. Indo-Saracenic architecture, Sufism, Sikhism and several other cultural features sprang to life because of the Muslim impact. Indian civilization became more complex because many more diverse elements entered into its composition. In fact, one may fancy that, though the advent of other influences was a disastrous event for the synthesis that had already been achieved, there was a secret impulsion in the seed-bed of Indian civilization to be more and more composite with the passage of centuries. The disturbance of the ancient pattern might have led to a period of chaos during the Middle Ages. But it was a chaos which lived side by side with a new-forming cosmos.

The medieval phase was about to achieve its own synthesis when other cultural elements—as widely different from the new medieval ones as from the ancient—came in, making a bid for a new complexity. The western impact through the British kindled the intellect and imagination of Indians and vivified and enriched Indian civilization, making it more composite, and brought about a veritable renaissance. Modern Indian civilization is still forming itself, though the outline of the new integration is faintly visible even today. It was this emergent pattern that bewildered Lord Curzon, the hard-boiled imperialist, when he remarked:

> There is no doubt that a sort of quasi-metaphysical ferment is going on in India, strangely conservative and even reactionary. The ancient philosophies are being exploited; and their modern scribes and professors are increasing in number and fame. What is to come out of this strange amalgam with European ideas thrown as an outside ingredient into the crucible—who can say?

The medieval and modern phases have to be viewed in this perspective, if the continuity and significance of Indian civilization are to be assessed correctly. Ancient Indian civilization did not disintegrate. It was reconstituting itself and forming itself anew during its medieval and modern phases.

Unity and complexity are the two features that have characterized Indian culture through the centuries. The complexity grew so multitudinous during India's weak periods that the sense of unity almost disappeared. This happened during the final phase of the struggle for empire in ancient India: 1000-1300 A.D. Similarly, an artificial unity was stamped on her abounding variety by an alien conqueror during the British regime, and an anamic uniformity was achieved in the place of a living and radiant unity. It was only during her peak periods of glory, as under the Mauryas, Asoka or Samudragupta, that Indian culture had its full flowering, retaining a living sense of unity as well as complexity. We are again passing through a phase in which our infinite variety seems to challenge and dominate our sense of unity. But our constitution is our Noah's Ark and one feels confident that it will be the nucleus round which a new and living sense of national unity will grow.

7

The Essentials of Modern Indian Culture

Any worthwhile cultural pattern attaches great importance to the dynamism and vitality of social, political, and economic growth. Among the early cultures, the Greek and Roman cultural systems stood, in addition, for the development of the rational, ethical, and aesthetic faculties in man. Asia, however, has also pursued the spiritual quest. Saints and mystics have always been held in greater esteem than any other type of person in Asia.

Speaking of India, spirituality—not an anaemic but a dynamic and all-embracing spirituality—has been the dominant strain in her culture from its very dawn. Ancient Indian culture stood for an infinite variety of symbols and rituals. But it never refrained from stressing the unity of the Divine that lay at the root. The fine arts were valued in ancient India primarily for their capacity to reveal something of the beauty and sublimity of the Divine. Literature was studied intensely because it expressed with remarkable subtlety the varying terms of the Inner Self. Coming to polity and governance, the king in ancient India was regarded as an instrument of the Divine. He was the trustee of the well-being and culture of his people. His cardinal duty was to protect *dharma*. Within this social framework, the main business of each individual was to evolve spirituality according to his *swabhava* or the law of his being and *swadharma*, his station in life which defined his duties for him.

All cultural systems were assumed to have a cycle of four phases in common. These were the four *Yugas* or epochs. During the *Satya Yuga* or the phase of truth, culture was a living reality permeating the whole of society, with no hiatus between ideals and their applications. No shadow fell between word and deed, though it was a stage of large and loose formation. The *Krita Yuga* was the stage in which the forms and rhythms were fixed and *Dwapara Yuga* the stage in which life was conventionalized to a great extent. But conventions did not lose their inner meaning and significance. The *Kali Yuga* was the stage of dissolution. The symbol here almost strangled what it symbolized and the flesh imprisoned spirit. In this phase, a culture died if it could not remould itself. But it could discard its outworn conventions and throw away its petrified ideas, it could resuscitate itself and go back again from the end to the beginning—the glory of a new dawn of truth.

We are passing through the fourth phase of our cultural cycle today.

> *Things fall apart. The centre does not hold.*
> *Mere anarchy is loosed upon the world.*

There came a time when the variety of religions developed into an irreconcilable diversity. Literature and the arts showed signs of degeneration. They spoke of the flesh with a fatal sense of fascination even when flesh figured only as a symbol of spirit—as in the sculptures of Khajuraho or in the rhythms and images of Jayadeva's *Geeta Govinda*. In the political sphere, social awareness, which had produced great administrators and warriors, was lost and brute selfishness prevailed often to the exclusion of even the bare minimum of decency. Indian culture was at its lowest ebb when this happened.

The reawakening, which was so badly needed, came from the West. We had dwindled into a kingdom of puppets full of rehearsed responses, as in Tagore's opera, experiencing no thrill, no joy in life, till the West came like the charming and dancing flute-player, put every one off his guard, swept them off their feet, and made the crowd, the king, and queen dance and sing for joy. The soul of India responded deeply to this call of the West, for it corresponded closely to what was already there, but had grown inert. There was the glorious outburst of the Indian Renaissance and a succession of prophets who rediscovered the ancient Truth in a new garb, aspect by aspect, and layer by layer. This process, I think, is now complete. The architects of India's destiny have evolved the integral philosophy of modern Indian culture during the last century and a half the blueprint of her new mansion. We now require engineers that can build it and people who can live in it, being mindful of their great privilege.

II

In what manner did India benefit by her contact with the West? In the last analysis it stimulated the Indian people to carry into all spheres of life, the full and unlimited sense of India's highest spirit and knowledge. As Sri Aurobindo has said: "If we do that, we shall find that the best of what comes to us, draped in occidental forms, is already implied in our own ancient wisdom and has there greater spirit behind it, a profounder truth and self-knowledge and the capacity of a will to nobler and more ideal formations." India borrowed a number of modern literary forms from the West, forms that had been evolved during the period of the European Renaissance and after. The method and instrumentation of inductive research, which had partly travelled from India to Europe, returned to India, bringing with it its more ample and modern achievements—the fascinating discoveries and inventions of European science. European industrialization, with its twin products of capitalism and socialism, also came to India. In the political sphere, the British impact ushered into India the press, the platform, and the processes of agitation and democracy.

The highway which took India from her medieval to her modern phase is marked, as it were, by convenient milestones in the form of great personalities. The first of these was Raja Ram Mohun Roy who advocated the gospel of reason and stressed the imperative need for social justice and religious reform. He had often expressed a wish to get inscribed on his tomb a maxim from Sa'di: "The true way of serving God is to do good to man." In a letter written to a friend on 18 August 1820, he wrote: "The struggles are not merely between the reformers and anti-reformers, but between liberty and oppression throughout the world, between justice and injustice, and between right and wrong." Regarding *suttee*, he wrote: "The advocates of concremation have been consequently driven to the necessity of taking refuge in *usage*, as justifying both suicide and female murder, the most heinous of crimes." While upholding reason and the promotion of a more liberal and enlightened system of instruction, embracing Mathematics, Natural Philosophy, Chemistry, Anatomy, etc., he wrote in his letter to the Governor-General: "If it had been intended to keep the British nation in ignorance of real knowledge, the Baconian philosophy would not have been allowed to displace the system of the schoolmen which was the best calculated to perpetuate ignorance. In the same manner the Sanskrit system of education would be the best calculated to keep this country in darkness, if such had been the policy of the British legislature." Ram Mohun Roy was the morning star of the Indian Renaissance. While he realized the value of the Indian heritage, he was also deeply aware of the new gifts that Europe had to give, the like of which were there before in India but had dimmed on the nation's memory for a long time.

Though he came later in point of time, Swami Dayanand Saraswati goes with Ram Mohun Roy. This is not so merely for the reason that each of them helped to found a *samaj*—*Brahmo* and *Arya*. Both strived hard to reform their religion and purge it of superstition and error. Both were fearless social reformers and seekers of truth. Unlike Ram Mohun Roy, Swami Dayanand never came under Western influence. Much less did he receive any Western education. But from his study of the Vedas alone, Swami Dayanand was able to perceive that true Hinduism or the Vedic religion was free from evils like idol-worship, the caste system, child marriage, enforced widowhood, and untouchability. He condemned them roundly and courted terrible persecution in the process. As H.B. Sarda says in his introduction to the Dayanand Commemoration Volume (Ajmer, 1933): "Swami Dayanand set to work to free India from untruth, superstition and the worship of false gods and, through India, the whole human race." "And though I was born in Aryavarta (India)," says Swami Dayanand in the *Satyarth Prakash,* "and still live in it, yet just as I do not defend the falsehoods of the religions prevailing in this country but expose them fully, in like manner I deal with the religions of other countries and their supporters. I treat the foreigners in the same way as my own countrymen so far as the elevation of the human race is concerned."

That he stood for the gospel of reason like Ram Mohun Roy is clear from Swami Dayanand's own statement: "The world is fettered by the chain forged by superstition and ignorance.

I have come to snap asunder the chain and to set slaves at liberty. It is contrary to my mission to have people deprived of their freedom."

This championing of reason and the rationalization of religion was traced to the Veda as Swami Dayanand interpreted it. As Sri Aurobindo says, "He seized justly on the Vedas as India's Rock of Ages and had the daring conception to build on what his penetrating glance perceived in it, a whole nationhood. Ram Mohun Roy, that other great soul and puissant worker...stopped short at the Upanishads. Dayanand looked beyond and perceived that our true original seed was the Veda." It may be that Swami Dayanand's original commentary may not be widely accepted as the definitive word on the Veda. But it was, as Sri Aurobindo says, "an act of grandiose intellectual courage to lay hold upon this scripture, defaced by ignorant comment and oblivion of spirit, degraded by misunderstanding to the level of an ancient document of barbarism, and to perceive in it its real worth as a scripture."

Tagore pays Swami Dayanand a handsome tribute, saying that he was a great path-maker in modern India, through the bewildering tangles of creeds and practices, leading the Hindus to a simple and rational life of devotion to God and service to mankind. Sri Aurobindo calls him a very soldier of light, a warrior in God's world, a sculptor of men and institutions, a bold and rugged victor of the difficulties which matter presents to spirit. His personality leaves an indelible impression of "spiritual practicality".

Sri Rama Krishna Paramahamsa and Swami Vivekananda constitute the next blessed pair. Their achievements are world renowned. It fell to the lot of an unlettered worshipper of Kali, an avatar, as it were, who came down for this very purpose to establish the two-fold unity that was the very essence of Hinduism: the unity that underlay the manifold paths pres-

cribed by yoga for God-realization, walking each one of them
on his own feet and proving to the world that they led to the
same destination; and the essential unity of all religions professed by mankind. Tolerance was only a corollary based on
this deep and underlying unity. The parables that fell from
Sri Rama Krishna's lips were like the parables of the Buddha
and Christ. There was in them an astonishing clarity and
illumination. It is only fitting that his recorded conversations
should have been published as his *Vachana Veda*. Sri Rama
Krishna's next great contribution in the service of humanity
was Swami Vivekananda himself.

Swami Vivekananda was the great apostle of spirit and its
flaming warrior. An indomitable love of the glories of spirit,
a pure and candid recognition of the importance and indis-
pensability of matter for a life of spirit, a spontaneous union
of what has been called (by Romain Rolland) contemplation
and action in his own personal life, a total adherence to the
truth that the service of the lowliest and the lost is the service
of God and an ardent and unquenchable passion for a regenerate India as the destined instrument for the service and spiritual
transformation of humanity: these were the noble ideas that
inspired him in the brief but glorious saga of his life. He saw
clearly how India and the West had to reinforce each other.
In India the quality of Rajas is almost absent; the same is
the case with Sattva in the West. It is certain, therefore,
that the real life of the Western world depends upon the
influx from India, of the current of Sattva or transcendenta-
lism; and it is also certain that unless we overpower
our Tamas by the opposite tide of Rajas, we shall never gain
any worldly good or welfare in this life.[1]

[1] *Complete Works of Swami Vivekananda*, Vol. IV, Birth Centenary Edition,
Mayavati, 1963, p. 408.

We then come to another illustrious name, that of Sri Aurobindo. The work that he did was unique even in a period of supreme unicities. His great collaborator in many of his supreme achievements was the Mother, Madame Mira Richard, known as the Divine Mother in Sri Aurobindo Asram in Pondicherry. It was under her fostering care and in the benign presence of Sri Aurobindo that this unique laboratory of the spirit grew up in Pondicherry. It was she who started the Sri Aurobindo International Education Centre as a memorial to Sri Aurobindo and launched the ship of Auroville which the UNESCO has recognized as a nucleus for the coming together of humanity in a storm-tossed world. The external drama of Sri Aurobindo's life up to the moment that he left for Pondicherry in 1910 is an epic of heroic struggle that held embryonically, as it were, Gandhi's programme for the liberation of India—its doctrine of passive resistance and *swadeshism*. The internal drama of his life at Pondicherry was a greater and more daring epic that finds expression in one of the world's great epics—Sri Aurobindo's *Savitri*. How shall we sum up the vast achievement of Sri Aurobindo, the fearless leader, the great poet, the philosopher of an unparalleled synthesis, the compassionate master, sage and prophet? He was the first to present comprehensively a philosophy which encompasses the twin poles of spirit and matter and points to the transformation of the individual and collective life of humanity into the Life Divine as the supreme goal and not merely the extinction of the self into a blank and featureless *nirvana*. His philosophy envisaged this on the basis of the triune principle—existence, consciousness, and bliss, *sachidananda*. It was on this solitary foundation that he built the entire metaphysical structure. Each human faculty had its own contribution to make to the rearing of this edifice— faith and reason, intellect and emotion, will and intuition.

The logic of the finite and the logic of the infinite moved together in this orchestral harmony. What is more, the philosophy was based on his own spiritual realizations or *siddhis*—the psychic realization, the realization of the static and dynamic Divine; his realization of the Supreme or *Purushottam* Consciousness while at Pondicherry and the supramental *maha siddhi*. The evolutionary ascent will not end with men but proceed through all the overhead planes to the supramental itself and a gnostic brotherhood will be formed which will be the definite nucleus for transforming the mind, life, and body of humanity as a whole. In order to achieve this, Sri Aurobindo evolved his own system of integral yoga and the Asram became the centre of this activity. It was in the light of integral yoga that a new system of education, physical exercise, co-education, and the pursuit of individual *sadhana*, and community living were organized.

Another major contribution of Sri Aurobindo was the series of seminal writings that he gave to the world on the predicament and destiny of man. The white radiance of his philosophy and vision burst into prismatic colours in its dissemination through various forms of literature. It is presented in its pristine philosophic purity in *Life Divine*. In its application to psychology and yoga this philosophic vision yields *The Synthesis of Yoga*. Turning to history, it results in *The Foundations of Indian Culture*. *The Human Cycle* and *The Ideal of Human Unity* are the products of its projection into sociology and political science. *The Secret of the Veda* reveals its application in the field of indology and philology. In his *Essays on the Gita* and writings on the Upanishads, he opened up strikingly new paths to a study of the ancient texts. If *The Future Poetry* is his profoundly original contribution to literary criticism and literary history, he also propounds a new theory of education in his book on the subject and his philosophic

70

essays and, above all, his letters offer illuminating comments on a variety of subjects, particularly psychology, yoga and poetry. I have not referred to his creative output—the quintessential lyrics, the lyric and narrative poetry, the translations, the plays and the two epics. The range of all these writings is as astonishing as their depth and insight. In many ways, Sri Aurobindo was the Vyasa of modern India.

In G.K. Gokhale and Lokamanya Tilak, we have another pair of patriots of genius. Tilak contributed to the cultural as well as political reawakening. As has been well said, he was the father of Indian revolution. He struck out new paths in political agitation, education, institution-building, journalism, nation-building, and indology. Gokhale, his contemporary and compeer, founder of the Servants of India Society, represented the unfoldment of the renaissance in a new direction. He stood for the spirit of liberalism and parliamentary democracy. His participation in the proceedings of executive and legislative bodies was characterized by a remarkable purity of motive, ardent patriotism, and limpidity of speech. Gokhale was modest and knew his place in Indian history. He said in 1907: "It will, no doubt, be given to our countrymen of future generations, to serve India by successes. We, of the present generation, must be content to serve mainly by our failures". According to C.P. Ramaswamy Aiyar, Gokhale became, through his consummately skilful and persuasive debates and disourses in the Bombay Legislative Council and the Imperial Legislative Council, for over a decade "the acknowledged and accredited leader of non-official Indian opinion". His constitutionalism and liberalism were not a bed of roses. They exacted from him elaborate and painful toil. "Patriotism by itself," said Gokhale, "is not enough. It is a noble powerful exalted emotion. It needs to be directed into useful fruitful channels. That can be done only if every worker prepared himself by ardous study, by patient survey of the realities of Indian life, and by appreciation on the spot of the varieties of factors involved in each particular case."

His integrity was unquestionable. When his informants had not the courage to stand by the letters that they wrote to him while he was in England and he had to withdraw the charges that he had made against the Bombay Government regarding their mishandling of the plague situation in Poona, Gokhale did not hesitate to tender a public apology. In a statement issued to the Press, he said:

> I have no doubt about the ultimate verdict on my conduct. ... Trials and troubles, accepted in the right spirit, only chasten and elevate. All that is necessary for me to do is to go on doing my duty, whether it be sunshine or shade. Public duties, undertaken at the bidding of no man, cannot be laid down at the desire of any one. Whether one works on a higher plane or a lower one is a matter comparatively of small importance. One is always glad of the approbation by the public of what one has done. It is an object of legitimate satisfaction; it is also more—it is a source of strength and encouragement; and, moreover, in this country, it constitutes the only reward in public life. But it is not the highest purpose of existence nor nearly the highest. If it comes—to use the words of Herbert Spencer—'well; if not, well also, though not so well'.

Here is a leaf taken out of the golden age of English prose, matching it on its own ground, in rhythm, in terms of expression and substance. This moral fervour, this loftiness of purpose, Gokhale carried into everything that he said and did. As P.N. Sapru says: "Gokhale spiritualized politics even as Jefferson and Abraham Lincoln did." In the words of

D.B. Mathur: "Gokhale handed down to Gandhi the legacy of spiritualization of public life, unity of means and ends, secularism, a deep-rooted sense of national mission, and faith in peace, justice, conciliation and progress." He became to his countrymen a shining example of an ideal parliamentarian with an unshaken faith in parliamentary democracy and a singular purity of motive in his championship of public causes.

Gokhale's integrity, sincerity, and talent had almost drawn Gandhiji into the charmed circle of his disciples. But his most distinguished follower was the Rt. Hon'ble Srinivas Shastri, the silver-tongued orator of the British empire. He achieved even greater fame than his master. The cultivation of parliamentary democracy on a national scale was a new experiment in India. But Gokhale and Shastri showed how this outlandish institution could take root in Indian soil. Their achievements made Indians realize that they could shine in this field as well.

Gandhiji and Vinoba can be taken up next. An illumined humanist, a spiritual experimentalist claiming no finality for his conclusions, Gandhiji, who became the father of the Indian Republic, sacrificed no principle to gain a political advantage. Truth was infinitely dearer to him than his Mahatmaship which was purely a burden. He knew the straight and narrow path and he rejoiced to walk on it. Truth was God. And he saw truth and love were the obverse and reverse of the same coin. He found beauty in truth and through truth. "Seek Truth," said Gandhiji, "and beauty and goodness will be added unto you."

Gandhiji was both idolator and iconoclast. He endeavoured to raise workers as co-partners with capitalists, for he sought to destroy, not capitalists, but capitalism. A classless society was his ideal too. But he would welcome communism only if it came without any violence. Socialism was essentially identical with the Upanishadic doctrine—all this is the house of God. Land should belong to him who works on it. If equal distribution was not possible, we should at least achieve equitable distribution.

He regarded an enlightened democracy as the finest thing in the world. But Swaraj would be an absurdity if the majority did not respect the opinion and action of the minority.

Gandhiji thought that the industrial civilization of the West was "satanic" because it was driven madly by an urge for exploitation. He thought that this civilization would destroy itself. What he objected to was the craze for machinery that turned machinery into a snake-hole which might contain from one to a hundred snakes. Heavy machinery for work of public utility had a place; but it should be owned by the State and used for the good of the people. After all, handicrafts and honest labour would remain when the achievements of the machine age would have disappeared.

Gandhiji made the doctrine of non-violence also peculiarly his own. War, he said, was an evil as everyone knew. The super powers should practice non-violence and earn universal gratitude. If an individual did not have the courage to be non-violent, he should preferably cultivate the act of killing and being killed rather than flee from danger in a cowardly manner. If one resorts to *satyagraha*, this should be done without ill-will and in a law-abiding manner. The non-co-operator should be guided by his search for truth, have the capacity to suffer any hardships and try to conquer untruth by truth, by expressing the voice of conscience in the national life. Non-cooperation should be a protest against participation in evil and have its roots in love. As for fasts, there can be no real fast without prayer.

There might have been societies in which the law of the jungle prevailed. The rule of law prevails in modern society. But in the ideal society of Gandhiji's dreams, love and law would be one. Nationalism should be based on broad and spiritual foundations. Gandhiji observed that he himself would prefer truth and non-violence to India's liberty: "I would prefer that India perished rather than that she won freedom at the sacrifice of truth."

I have attempted in the preceding paragraphs a summary of some of the cardinal ideas that inspired Gandhiji's programme of cultural and political action. He took over part of his philosophy from some of his great predecessors—Sri Rama-krishna's idea of the unity of all religions, Vivekananda's championship of the weak and fallen and his notion of India's supreme position among nations in the world of spirit. From Sri Aurobindo he took over the concept of nationalism rooted in spiritual values and items in the programme for political action such as passive resistance and *swadeshism*. Reality he experienced as truth rather than as *sachidananda*. He was an illuminated humanist rather than a *siddha*, a realized soul. Nor had Gandhiji's philosophy the comprehensiveness or the inter-relation of parts that are so marvellously present in Sri Aurobindo's writings and utterances.

But Gandhiji's was a working philosophy which was fairly coherent and consistent, indicating lines of development and progress both for the individual and the collectivity. And its uniqueness lay in the fact that it was made operative not only in Gandhiji's own personal life but in the life of a whole people in spite of their bewildering diversity. His experiments with truth were personal and, at the same time, made on a nation-wide scale. This was Gandhiji's unique role and his great opportunity. The nation was totally involved in his experiments since he had identified himself with it. Gandhiji was thus able to write a great chapter in the history of humanity by employing, for the first time, a philosophy of spirit as a programme for winning the political freedom of India. The man, the moment, and the milieu were supremely matched with each other.

Another major achievement of Gandhiji was the fact that during his long years of leadership, whether within or without the Congress, he drew within his magic circle iron men like Sardar Patel, idealists like Pandit Nehru, astute men of the world like C. Rajgopalachari, simple and devoted leader-lieutenants like Dr Rajendra Prasad, and poets like Sarojini Naidu, so that when freedom came, there were seasoned leaders in all fields and in all the province of India to take over the administration. Gandhiji had multiplied himself at many levels and carried the message of economic, political, cultural and spiritual freedom to the commonest man in the street.

Vinoba Bhave, Gandhiji's chosen disciple in the realm of spirit, stood on the atlantean shoulders of his master and saw farther ahead. He summed up the Gandhian gospel neatly in his philosophy of Sarvodaya, walked in the footprints of his master from one end of India to the other, pleading for, and succeeding here and there in bringing about an equitable distribution of land, insisting on *dan,* and sincere and spontaneous self-sacrifice. It was only in this way that red revolution and the spilling of blood could be avoided. C.F. Andrews called Vinoba one of the few pearls in the Wardha Ashram, one who came not to be blessed by the Ashram, but to bless it. This "god who gave away land" and "looted people with love" gave a new dimension to Gandhian thought and constructive activity and brought about, as Shri Sriran Narayan has said, a "socio-economic" renaissance, a minor revolution in the minds of men. As Gandhiji wrote to Vinoba in 1932, the fiery ordeal Vinoba was going through would build a bridge between heaven and earth. But the forces let loose by the struggle for power in independent India were too strong to allow this psychological revolution to last for any length of time. Vinoba also extended the Gandhian gospel by making it include science as well as spirituality. Pandit Nehru used this phrase as the watchword for new India.

Coming to the last pair—Pandit Nehru and Tagore—Nehru was the westernized disciple of a typically eastern saint. If Gandhiji were to be considered as Plato, Nehru would be his Aristotle. Since the days of Asoka there was hardly any idealist statesman except Akbar who had the opportunity to implement his ideas and inject them into a whole people. His greatest work was done as a rebel. But he was also a great prime minister. Authorship was only one aspect of his multi-faceted personality. He wrote his *Autobiography*, *Discovery of India*, and *Glimpses of World History* when in prison. Life was greater in his eyes than literature. On his whirlwind tours in India both as a rebel and as a prime minister, he loved to speak to the "masses" of India. He would have liked to be a teacher and this is how he satisfied his teaching impulse by trying to "educate our masters".

Influenced as he was by Karl Marx as much as by Gandhiji, Nehru had an innate preference for humanism and socialism. He had his spiritual longings too, as is seen in his glowing tribute to the Ganges in his Will and Testament and in several other colourful paragraphs in his writings. But his agnostic ambivalence was part of the Hamlet-like indecision which made him so lovable and so vulnerable at the same time. Nehru said: "I am half eastern, I am half western. Probably I am more western than eastern. I find myself out of place everywhere and at home nowhere." But he could also say in his Will, in which he expressed the desire for the submergence of a handful of his ashes into the Ganga at Allahabad to be carried to the great ocean that washes India's shore:

"The Ganga especially, is the river of India. She has been

a symbol of India's age-long culture and civilization, ever-changing, ever-flowing, and yet ever the same Ganga.... I am proud of that great inheritance that has been and is ours and I am conscious that I too, like all of us, am a link in that unbroken chain which goes back to the dawn of history in the immemorial past of India.

Three great achievements stand out to his credit as the Prime Minister. The gigantic five-year plans that he initiated put India, in spite of all limitations, firmly on the path of modernization and industrialization. The village *panchayats* that he conceived and established in all the Indian states are still functioning in an experimental way. But when they take root and form, they are sure to be the backbone of the world's greatest democracy. Thirdly, his advocacy of *pancha shila*, peaceful co-existence and non-alignment, raised India's status and made her impact perceptible in the eyes of the world. He even had his vision of a united world:

I have no doubt in my mind that the World Government must and will come, for there is no remedy for the world's sickness. The machinery for it is not difficult to devise. It can be an extension of the federal principle, a growth of the idea underlying the United Nations giving each national unit freedom to fashion its destiny according to its genius, but subject always to the basic covenant of the World Government.

I have bracketed Nehru with Tagore rather than with Gandhiji, for they shared several things in common. Nehru had a passion for beauty, for the red rose, for literature, and the creative arts. In spite of his mystical perceptions, Tagore was also something of a humanist, the advocate of the Religion

78

of Man and the worshipper of *Jeevan Debata*. Both Tagore and Nehru were nationalists and internationalists. As Nehru himself said: "I was very much in contact with Gandhiji and he affected me tremendously. And yet my mind was a little more in tune with Tagore." He observed again: "Gandhi came on the public scene in India like a thunder-bolt shaking us all, and like a flash of lightning which illumined our minds and warmed our hearts; Tagore's influence was not so sudden or so earth-shaking for India's humanity. And yet, like the coming of the dawn in the mountains, it crept on us and permeated us."

Tagore was the first to express in his creative as well as critical writings, the new aesthetics of the Indian Renaissance, an aesthetics that comprehended Eastern as well as Western terms and yet was essentially of its own place and time. He expressed it in a number of literary forms and attained the hall-mark of excellence in each one of them. His Nobel Laureate-ship was, in a great measure, responsible for the wide diffusion of his impact at home and abroad and this made him the symbol and spokesman of the new literary resurgence in India. He spoke longingly of Universal Man and Santiniketan and Sriniketan, which were grandly conceived and designed, built up and maintained a really national and international atmosphere of learning and creative education for a long time. Guru Dev Tagore became the poet and prophet of New India.

There were many other celebrated personalities that helped lead India on her path of self-finding and self-exceeding. Swami Ram Tirth and Bhagawan Ramana Maharshi; Dr S. Radha-krishnan, who won for Indian philosophy world audiences and became one of its most brilliant exponents; Maulana Azad, and Dr Zakir Husain; the great scientists of India including J.C. Bose and C.V. Raman; leaders like Dadabhai Naoroji, the Grand Old Man of India, Pherozeshah Mehta, C.R. Das, and M.N. Roy who changed over from communism to scientific humanism. One can think of an unending roll-call of honour. But here I have concerned myself with great men who have contributed one vital constituent or the other to the value culture that has emerged in India during the nineteenth and twentieth centuries. The essentials of modern Indian culture have been mostly formulated by the leaders whose work I have reviewed. And it is time to recapture these essentials briefly.

III

The value-system within which this culture functions may be summed up in this way: each individual has to be a conqueror of his own self and master of his environment. Personal salvation is barely half the goal.

Spirit and Matter are both divine. The materialist's affirmation is only half truth. So is the ascetic's denial. The body is not to be despised. Nor is it to be glorified at the expense of spirit. The marriage of earth and heaven is the ideal to strive for, for heaven is our father even as the earth is our mother.

The culture we evolve has to satisfy all the faculties in man: faith and reason, intellect and emotion, will and intuition. An excess of the instinctive life is like living in lush grass. An excess of the intellect makes a desert of one's life. To be excessively emotional is like living beneath a waterfall. A life of mere action is a step in the dark. The intuition has to be awakened and trained to perceive reality. Instinct and emotion, faith, reason and intellect will have to be subordinated to and transfigured by it. Beauty, truth, goodness, love and power have all to be cultivated if life, the rose with five-coloured petals, has to yield all its secrets.

Evil is an aberration, a deformity in this universe. The world is not to be shunned as transitory and evil. It has to be transformed so as to reflect fully the light of the Supreme.

A regenerate man within an ideal society is the ultimate goal and destiny of the earth. The highest individual achievement is to be one with the Supreme, live in the constant presence of the Supreme or be His puissant channel, living in the Truth-Consciousness. The highest collective achievement lies in realizing the ideal of human brotherhood. Mankind is slowly moving towards it, having experimented with theocracy, oligarchy, monarchy, democracy, and the dictatorship of the proletariat.

The medieval mystic believed only in the infinity of spirit. The modern scientist believes in the infinity perceived by the physical senses and the intellect. The highest meaning of life is open to us only when we accept the three factors of existence —the soul, the World Soul, and the Transcendent Divine. India had forgotten the middle term during her period of stagnation. It was the Western impact that helped her correct herself.

I have presented in the preceding paragraphs the essence extracted from the writings of Ram Mohun Roy, Swami Dayanand, Sri Ramakrishna, Swami Vivekananda, Sri Aurobindo, the Mother, Gandhiji, Vinoba Bhave, and Tagore. Gokhale, Srinivas Shastri, and Nehru were more preoccupied with the social and political aspects of the culture. Again, the seers from Ram Mohan Roy to Tagore did not quite use the language that I have used. Ram Mohun Roy was a unitarian and would not have countenanced the description of reality as triune. Swami Vivekananda would have preferred the *advaitic* terminology. Gandhiji would not have ventured beyond the description that God is Truth and Love. Each one of them has his individual idiom. But apart from the variations, which are dialectical and metaphysical, the spirit of their writings could be said to affirm the substance of what has been stated in the preceding paragraphs.

In the economic sphere, India believes in an equitable

distribution of land, promotion of small scale industries, nationalization of major industries, and a classless society neither rooted in violence nor arising out of it. Politically speaking, a socialist republic, fostered through parliamentary democracy and village panchayats, is the destination.

The policy of nonalignment and peaceful co-existence should prevail in the sphere of international relations. A few political parties may differ from what has been stated with regard to some particulars in the programme. But the centrist view stands more or less as I have summed it up. Many of our twelve thinkers have commented on this aspect, except perhaps Swami Dayanand, Sri Ramakrishna, and Swami Vivekananda.

In the social sphere, there is general agreement that there should be no discrimination between man and man, on the basis of caste, language, region, colour, or class. All the twelve thinkers have declared with one voice that such iniquities must go. It may be difficult to eradicate the divisions that exist. Nor does it matter whether they exist or disappear so long as they do not militate against the fundamental human decencies and considerations of merit in public life. Indeed, variations of community, region, and language may bring charm and variety, once the basic unity and value system have been established. A just and balanced thinking in national terms on all these matters has to be actively taught and practised till this is achieved.

In the sphere of religion, there was a tremendous revolt against superstitious and ignorant customs from the days of Ram Mohun Roy and Swami Dayanand. All the twelve thinkers worked for religious reform, though it is far form accomplished even today. It may even be desirable to form a group to draw up a modern *smriti* and *dharma shastra*, for that was very probably how the old *smritis* and *shastras* were compiled. The religious programme for each day for every individual has to be revised in accordance with the needs and exigencies of our times; what exists was prepared for other times and other conditions. There is hardly any religion left today, whether for daily life or for festive or sacred occasions, for lack of religious reform which is in tune with our new social structure.

If the essence of religion has not been active in our daily lives, its mere name and form have played havoc in our social and political life. Sectarianism and communalism have eaten into our vitals. This is where the doctrine of secularism should hold sway. Secularism need not mean that all religions should be neglected and allowed to rot and decay. Since religions are going to stay, they have to be rationalized, revised, and revivified sooner rather than later. At the same time, the doctrine of secularism has to be fostered and asserted firmly so that a programme and an ideology, that were meant for promoting individual and domestic culture, are not projected into our social and political life, clashing with other religious programmes and ideologies.

Lastly, in the cultural sphere, there has been an outburst of thrilling creative activity all round. Literature and the fine arts woke up from a torpor about a century ago, literature awaking earlier than its sister arts. The only danger now is that technique may supersede vision instead of being its astral body. If we have not grasped the fundamentals of our own culture, we are likely to be swept off our feet by fashions that come from elsewhere, fashions rooted in value-systems that we have not fully grasped. It is better to cling to our roots and readjust or multiply them, if more and other roots are needed, instead of being rootless and attempting to join our stems to roots that thrive in other soils.

Our education system needs a drastic reorientation. It is the one sphere of life that has not yet renewed itself with each stage of our renaissance. It has therefore clogged national progress. But there are signs that here too things have begun to move.

I am aware of the fact that, in all that I have said, I have concentrated on the work done by a few typical thinkers and prophets. More evidence for the conclusions drawn could be adduced from the writings of other great sons of India like Dadabhai Naoroji, Khan Abdul Ghafar Khan, Maulana Azad, and Dr Zakir Husain. The renaissance was a movement in which the entire nation was involved and the twelve steps that were taken in the formulation of her culture could be presented even from the point of view of each region in the country. The Indian Renaissance has to be evaluated from all angles so that the total picture of national resurgence and reorientation may emerge in a clearer outline. One will then be able to see vividly the unity that underlies the pattern. All the great communities in India were subjected to the same pressures, kindled and stimulated by the same formative influences. Their experiences were the same and the value-system formed on that basis will also naturally be the same.

I think that this unity of the renascent motif can be brought into clearer relief, if the representative thinking of each great community in the country were to be analyzed and presented in its evolution towards modernism. Buddhism, Islam, Christianity and Zoroastrianism, variations within the Indian fold like Jainism, Saivism, Virasaivism, Vaishnavism, Srivaishnavism, and Sikhism—all these religions and creeds have passed through the renascent phase. What is required is an authentic and detailed documentation of the unobtrusive transformation that has come over them, considerable in some cases and not inconsiderable in others.

A documentation of this kind is available for Islam in India. A book like Professor Aziz Ahmad's *Islamic Modernism in India and Pakistan* gives a vivid idea of the rethinking on

Islam during the renascent phase.

A distinction was made between the permanent and temporary injunctions of the Quran and a historical perspective introduced into the study of the Quran by the Aligarh School, including Amir Ali, who summed up the essential teachings of the Quran as "ethical humanism". Sufi quietism, which belittled worldly power and glory—a trend which had been accentuated in the Hindu fold by the doctrine of Maya—was relegated to a secondary place by the rising tide of modernism, the impact of which was first felt in the occidentalism, the rationalization of non-essential dogma and the historical scepticism present in the writings of Sir Sayyid Ahmad Khan. This kind of speculative modernism assumed a radical aspect in the writings of Chiragh Ali and an anti-traditionalist turn in the writings of Mursin Al-Mulk. Mumtaj Ali promoted the feminist movement. There was also a traditionalist revival launched by Nanotawi, Gangohi, and others of the Deoband seminary, comparable to the revivalist trends of the various *maths* and *peeths* in the Hindu fold. Mawdudi, with his theory of an Islamic theo-democracy, stood for an orthodox fundamentalism, regarding the later developments in Islam as a falling away from the golden age of the Prophet. This may, in a way, be compared with Dayanand Saraswati's Arya Samaj movement, harking back to the Vedas as the undefiled source of Hinduism. Shibli gave historiography a strong conservative colour of revivalism and Hali, in his narrative poetry, popularized political romanticism as Bankim Chandra Chatterji and Hari Narayan Apte did in their novels. Al-Afghani and Muhammad Ali led the various turns that the pan-Islamic movement took in India. Sindhi and Sihawarwi propounded their own theory of Islamic socialism.

Against this background of cultural and religious activity in the late nineteenth and early twentieth century, there arose two schools that had a great influence on Muslim opinion during the second quarter of this century. One was led by Iqbal who evolved the theory of Pakistan within the concept of multi-national neo-pan-Islamism. This was developed into a political movement by Jinnah. The other one was shaped by the exegetical eclecticism of Maulana Abul Kalam Azad who offered, as a solution, humanism in place of rationalism and a synthesis of traditionalism and modernism in place of pure speculation. He saw the basic unity of all religions and stood for a kind of religious universalism. In the political field, he favoured composite nationalism and cooperation with the Indian National Congress, a policy which was also supported by the leaders of the Deoband seminary and the more representative body called the Jamiyat al-Ulama-i Hind. This was also the stand of Dr Zakir Husain. He declared that Indian Muslims loved their country as much as any of their compatriots. They would not accept the complete loss of their cultural identity. They would like to be good Muslims as well as good Indians.

Similar accounts have yet to be presented from the point of view of various communities and regions in the country. These will help us form an integral view of modern Indian culture. This culture is not just an offspring of the West, though the West exercised a formative influence upon it. If we do not examine the roots of this culture in the ancient past and in its growth or decay during the Middle Ages, we shall not be able to grasp its full significance. What is worse, we shall harbour a superficial notion of it, unrelated to our heritage.

There are other schools of thought which take a different view of Indian culture. The humanist or Marxist will have nothing to do with Spirit and he would like to banish it from all serious discussion. In that case, the ancient and medieval Indian heritage will be bereft of a good part of its essential significance. It may be possible to isolate the economic, social, and political categories of Indian life and thought, and to be exclusively concerned with them. In that case we shall have only a fragmentary view of Indian culture. The central impulse that sustained these aspects of life is as important today as it was in the past. To seize upon Swami Vivekananda's championship of the poor and downtrodden, for example, and ignore his mystical philosophy would amount to misinterpreting him and the culture for which he stood. In my account of the essentials of modern Indian culture, I have tried to take to the high road, taking Indian culture as it stood, without bending it to the uses of one school of philosophy or the other. If the acceptance of spirit and all that it connotes implies adherence to a particular school, I should like to plead guilty to the charge, for Indian culture through the ages has itself been guilty of it.

IV

Dr Mulk Raj Anand says: "While it is obvious that India may be evolving a contemporary life concept of its own, it would be dishonest to proclaim it as anything like a finished thing and to pretend that it is any more than an unconscious tentative life-view, with many unresolved conflicts, challenges and contradictions in it."[2] He feels that all that can be claimed is that the direction of a new kind of humanist socialist civilization has been set, one that does not believe in violence and is not based on the fatalist hypothesis of ancient India.

Quite a few may think like me that this idea of a "humanist socialist civilization" describes only the surface of the reality we wish to achieve. One may feel, in fact, that this description leaps over the cardinal significance of Indian civilization for

[2]Mulk Raj Anand, *Is There a Contemporary Civilization?*, Asia, 1963, pp. 173-4.

the last four thousand years—its insistence on the full flowering of spirit in all spheres of life. A "humanist socialist civilization" can only be the end-product of a successful and centrally spiritual approach to life. Humanism and socialism can thrive only where there is, what Dr Anand himself calls "awareness of beauty", "the brotherhood of man through the affirmation of love" and "harmony with Nature". Western civilization is passing through a crisis because it has ignored these very essentials of the individual and collective life. Indian civilization has insisted through the ages that these values become accessible to man when his intuition is awakened, his inner eye opened, and he quickly realizes within his depths his unity with all created beings. This is the bedrock on which a humanist and socialist civilization can stand securely. "The application of imagination, reason and scientific method in all human undertakings" which Dr Anand advocates, is understandable but not adequate. If lasting results are to be achieved, love or intuition, which really is the soul-gaze of man, has to lead them to the desired transformation. When Dr Anand says that "man is, and becomes, what he wants by transforming Nature", he is making a statement which is in complete harmony with Indian metaphysical thought. This could be said without trying in detail to resolve the paradox of Destiny and Free Will.

Because Dr Anand does not accept the central import of Indian civilization, he is also not able to appreciate the integral vision unfolded by the Indian Renaissance. He stresses only the humanistic side of Raja Ram Mohun Roy, Tagore, Gandhi, and Nehru. But there were other outstanding prophets like Ramakrishna Paramahamsa, Swami Vivekananda and Dayanand Saraswati. Moreover, to see only the humanistic aspect of the personality of Ram Mohun Roy, Tagore, Gandhi and Nehru is not to see them whole or to assess fully their contribution to the rebuilding of India. There are several passages even in Nehru's writings that reveal his ambivalence, his passion for humanism, and his love of spirituality.

Dr Anand pays a handsome tribute to the Indian people for their comparative freedom from "wild fanaticism for war in a hate-ridden world." He confesses to having returned frequently to India "with a kind of nostalgia, which is not so much the wish for home as a quest for comparative calm in the world of irritation, fear and anger." And he admits the possibility that India "could become a kind of laboratory for the experiment of building a new kind of human society." In fact, one feels, after reading Dr Anand's book, that he is in revolt, not so much against spirituality itself as its abuse and misapplication during our period of stagnation, when the quest for individual salvation overshadowed the centrality of man and the concern of spirituality for the wise ordering of the collective life. Dr Anand's hope for "a new kind of human society in India" is also the hope that inspires another writer, Mrs Lila Ray, who remarks that, in India, "a new element has emerged, an element which reflects the essential unity of the human mind and gives rise to a broader humanism than the world has ever before sought to practise."[3]

I have spoken of the need for engineers to translate the blueprint prepared by the prophets of the renaissance into a concrete structure. In this context, no one has seen better the gap between the ideal and the real than Dr Mulk Raj Anand. He speaks with considerable resentment of the casteism, parochialism, communalism and linguism in twentieth-century India, the hiatus in our planning programme, the staggering growth of our population, our "inefficient, uninspired and almost heartless bureaucracy", the "practice of many bad habits

---

[3]*Equities,* Indian Institute of Culture, Bangalore, 1955, p. 76.

which are neither permitted by the old culture nor preferred by those who respect the principles of a new humanist life-view", the corruption of profit-makers and opportunist political leaders and the dual allegiance to God and Mammon and imitationism, commercialism, corruption, and vulgarity of the upper rank population of Bombay, Calcutta, Madras, and Delhi. He grows lyrical when he speaks of the mutual confidence among men, cooperation, respect and the sharing of burdens together that were the hallmark of our earliest primitive village republics. He draws a glowing picture of his utopia in which our seven hundred thousand villages could become the nuclei of a co-operative commonwealth, a basic panchayat democracy which avoids the pitfalls of the Western industrial civilization, using some of its techniques but without borrowing the profit system behind it.

This is a consummation which each one of us would like to strive for. The village republic that Dr Anand speaks of came in the wake of a philosophy of life that carried spirit into the daily lives of men. There has to be a similar upsurge in our lives today, if we desire a similar fulfilment.

Professor S. Abid Husain's book[4] is another interesting contribution to the literature on modern Indian culture. It is a stimulating survey and gives some interesting information about the medieval period. If Dr Anand stresses the humanistic element in culture, Professor Abid Husain sums up the general features of Indian culture. Since he thinks that these features are likely to remain the same ("even if the demands of the new age make a change inevitable, it can only be one of form, not of essence or character"), they may be examined in some detail.

Professor Husain thinks that the feeling of solitude

[4]*Indian Culture*, Asia, 1963.

on an Indian summer night, which makes one feel that there
is nothing in the infinite universe except oneself and the starspangled heavens, enables one to understand why, in India,
the capacity for contemplation and the sense of unity in diversity are the two most prominent characteristics of the Indian
mind. Again he says that, in this physical environment, hot
blood courses through the veins stimulating the emotions and
imagination fans the flame of passion further. Another assump-
tion that he makes is that the climate being mild and the
wants of the people few, the Indian mind is indifferent to economic effort. This results in a fatalistic trend. Because of the
regularity and continuity of seasons and other natural processes, the Indian mind tends to believe that the operation of
the moral law is quite as regular and continuous. On the whole,
Professor Husain thinks that all this endows the Indian
mind with a deep religious consciousness and encourages
not struggle but peace as an ideal, not self-assertion but self-
abnegation.

It is true that the Indian climate has, for the most part, an
enervating effect. But this could also be said about the climate
in some parts of the USA. I think the point cannot be
pressed too hard. For instance, the starspangled heavens which
kindle in one a sense of unity in diversity may, in another
mood or in another observer, deepen a sense of the diversity
that dwells in the unity. I agree with Professor Husain
when he says that "spirituality" has been the dominant trait of
the Indian mind through the centuries. But spirituality need
not necessarily rule out a balanced view of the good things
of the world. It is now widely recognized that the spirituality
of ancient India was not a world-shunning spirituality. It
permeated all life and sought to transfigure all activity by its
own pervasive touch. During the medieval period, when the
synthesis of the Hindu view of life had broken down, Islam

brought into India a new spiritual strength and vivifying force. It was the element of spirituality that led India, during the period of her Great Tradition, to cultivate all the sciences and arts, the sixty-four lores, making life opulent and turning it into a tryst of time and eternity. It also enabled the Indian people to build the great Mauryan, Gupta, and Moghul empires.

But a good part of Professor Husain's view is valid, though for another reason. There are the leaders of society who have the transfiguring vision. There is also the great mass of people who have to be introduced to this vision and stimulated to develop it as part of their own consciousness.

As Sri Aurobindo has said, the application of this vision in the collective life of Indian society was subjected to serious reserves. "Never sufficiently bold and thorough-going, it became more and more limited and halting when the life-force declined in her peoples." The significance of the Indian Renaissance lies in the fact that it has spelt out a dynamic and integral philosophy. What is now required is an effort, more determined than ever, to see that the Indian people assimilate the essence of this message in their own terms, individually and collectively. This would be the second phase of the Renaissance.

8

Indian Culture and Secularism

The integrative and disruptive forces in Indian society are themselves different from the problem areas in the life of our people; those like religion, language, and community. If these latter are interpreted in absolute terms and adhered to in an undiscerning manner, divisive forces are generated and great conflict can ensue. India has set before herself the ideal of a democratic republic and has been endeavouring to move steadily towards this goal. Because of her size and young age as a republic, she has been confronted with a number of problems. There are political problems like the one of relations between the Centre and the States and the reorganization of States; economic problems like the removal of disparities, proper balancing of agricultural and industrial sectors and the private and public sectors in Indian economy; social problems like the welding together of various ethnic groups into one nation through the absorption of tribal societies and the emancipation of the Harijans; educational problems like adult education, continuing education, and the transformation of a public that lives at different levels of culture into an enlightened republic; and cultural problems like those of linguistic unity in the midst of diversity, the autonomy of regional cultures under the aegis of a national culture and the maintenance of a steady process of continuity and change, balancing tradition with technological development.

There is much passion and argument in each one of these sectors at this stage of our evolution. Both passion and arguments frequently play a disruptive role, consciously or unconsciously. But the integrative forces are also steadily at work, insisting on the right balance of antinomies and detecting the reconciling principle that guides analysis towards synthesis. Tensions of this kind are natural in a developing country. They were not and are not unknown in Russia and the USA. Their reverberations have been heard in Canada and North Ireland. One has to continuously pave the way for the victory of the forces of integration over those of disruption.

One could venture the statement that the word "secular", as applied to an integrating or integrated society, refers to only two of these tensions: (1) The peaceful coexistence of diverse religious faiths in India, unaffected by any communal distrust or rancour. (2) The harmonious participation of the members of all castes, creeds and communities in the mainstream of national life, which includes our economic, social, legal, political, and cultural systems, as lawfully equal citizens. We may now examine whether the semantic history of the word "secular" holds forth any remedy for resolving these tensions.

The word "secular" has descended from the Latin adjective *saecularis* which comes from the Latin noun *saecul-um*. *Saecul-um* has two different meanings. Like the Sanskrit word, *Kala*, it is related to the concept of time and means "generation; age". Like the Sanskrit word, *sakala*, it is also related to the concept of space and means "the world". It also gradually acquires the meaning: "The world, particularly as opposed to the church". The multisemantic nature of what Owen Barfield has called Primitive Language is thus illustrated in a way in the word *Saeculum* which connotes time and space, two different aspects of reality, at the same time.

We are not concerned here with that meaning of the word "secular" which is associated with time and implies: "Of or belonging to an age or long period." This is the meaning detected in English for the first time around 1600 A.D. in phrases like "the secular games of ancient Rome." Gibbon uses the phrase "secular festival" for denoting "the hundredth birthday". The word also acquires the extended meaning: "Living or lasting for an age or ages". This is what we get in R.F. Burton's (1875 A.D.) reference to a "forest of secular trees" or Lowell's phrase, "the secular leisures of Methusaleh". This is supported by the scientific sense of the word in phrases like "the secular seasons of the earth" or "secular refrigeration", meaning "the periodical cooling and consolidation of the globe, from a supposed original state of fluidity from heat".

The meaning of the word *secular* "of or pertaining to the world" was prevalent in Christian Latin and this was first used to refer to the clergy "living in the world" and not in monastic seclusion like the "regular" and "religious" clergy. The phrase "secular arm" was used by Wyclif to refer to the civil power invoked by the church to punish offenders. The word gradually acquired the meaning, "belonging to the world and its affairs as distinguished from the church and religion." It meant something civil, lay or temporal, non-ecclesiastical, non-religious or non-sacred. Newman spoke of bishops involved in "secular occupations" and Tennyson said in *Queen Mary*: "A secular kingdom is but as the body lacking a soul." This is the meaning of the word with which we are chiefly concerned. It was gradually extended to all departments of human activity not concerned with or devoted to the service of religion—secular history, literature, art, architecture, music, plays, economic and political life, and education, as in J. Grant's statement: "These persons maintain that the public schools should be purely secular".

The second meaning of the word "secular", which is relevant to our discussion, is: "Of or belonging to the present or visible world, as distinguished from the eternal or spiritual world; wordly." The opposition between these two terms is presented vividly in a statement: "To the secular nothing is spiritual, and to the spiritual nothing is secular." There are several schools of thought which reject God and the spiritual life altogether and account for the evolution of the world and man purely in material terms, like Marxism and scientific humanism. They refuse to take any supra-rational factors into account; or they emphasize material well-being, collectively and individually, like utilitarianism. These are secular philosophies, as opposed to the mysticism of a Kabir or Berdyaev or Sri Aurobindo. The acceptance of such a philosophy which excludes any belief in the soul, immanence or transcendence leads to the formation of a wholly secular society. This may not be the end which India has in view for its own progressive evolution. Even in Russia, where a secular philosophy is elevated to the position of the philosophy of the State, a more liberal attitude has been perceptible towards religion though the Constitution of the USSR ensures full freedom for anti-religious, but not for religious, propaganda. India seeks to cultivate tolerance in the context of the coexistence of diverse religious societies and fraternties subscribing to different philosophies.

Another meaning of the word refers to a definitely professed system of belief promulgated by G.J. Holyoake (1817-1906). Secularism, as a doctrine, advocates that morality should be based solely on regard to the well-being of mankind in the present life, to the exclusion of all consideration drawn from belief in God or in a future state. Holyoake describes secularism as the practical philosophy of the people, expressing a certain positive and ethical element which the terms "sceptic" and "atheist" do not express. A number of secular societies were formed in various English towns, about the middle of the nineteenth century, to spread secularist opinions. Though this meaning is specialized and restricted to a particular doctrine, one can easily see that it has affinities with the second meaning of the word "secular": "Of or belonging to the present or visible world as distinguished from the eternal or spiritual world." Holyoake's secularism could also be subsumed under this head along with other secular philosophies.

A third meaning of the word has begun to emerge recently, though it may not have found its way to the dictionaries as yet. It is discernible in the writings of students of comparative religion and mystical philosophers. For example, Professor David Baily Harned, Chairman of the Department of Religious Studies at the University of Virgina, USA, says:

> Secularization can have three meanings. . . . Third, the word can also imply that the quest for the holy has become diffused beyond the normal precincts of the sacred or the religious. The dominance of functional norms and the development of institutional autonomy in the public realm and, on the other hand, the proliferation of private forms of religiosity, testify that this sort of secularization is a pervasive pheno- menon in the modern West.[1]

Professor Harned goes on to say that this kind of diffusion holds great and various dangers for the Christian tradition, for it may end up in a denial of the basic dogmas of Christian theology or, at least a diminution of their importance. In

---

[1]David Baily Harnee, *Grace and Common Life*, Punjab University, Patiala, 1970, p. 134.

another sense, however, he says that the diffusion is quite consonant with the tradition and largely inspired by it, for he sees no integral relation between the sacred and the holy and intimations of the holy are discovered precisely in the most ordinary and recurrent of experiences. He concludes: "In the precise sense of the diffusion of the quest for ecstasy beyond the realm of the conventionally sacred or religious, secularization is a proper and important product of Christianity."[2] He maintains that "religion" suggests that something dynamic is really static, that something protean is really uniform. He would prefer to discard the confusing distinctions between sacred and profane and between religious and secular to replace them by the categories of the holy and the human. As for the holy, it is said to be experienced primarily when old certainties dissolve and the self must strike out into *terra incognita*. Two contrasting moralities are mentioned, that of the man of sanctity concerned primarily with redeeming the times and contributing to the work of God and that of the secular man concerned primarily with building new and imaginary worlds for the delight of human sensibility, the one oriented first of all towards the holy and the other towards the expression of the capacities and possibilities of the self. And the conclusion is that both the man of sanctity and the secular man may have equal title to be called Christian.

This meaning of "secularization" is implied in Khalil Gibran's imaginative account of the life of Jesus Christ. This connotation, which restricts itself to the purely spiritual life of man, as distinguished from conformity to a given theological system, may be regarded as the secularization of the inner life to distinguish it from the negative secularism which may be said to consist in the denial of any discrimination made on the

[2]*Ibid.*, p. 136.

basis of caste and creed and between religion and religion. This kind of "secularization"—which is really spiritualization— is at the root of all mysticism which is the art or science of the spiritual life. Sri Aurobindo and Gandhiji have made it famous with reference to the Hindu heritage.

The other two meanings, which Professor Harned detects in the words "secular" and "secularization", are in line with the two central meanings we have already discussed. One is "the condition of the remainder of the world, after the holy has been identified with a particular sacred power or community". This kind of identification leads to hostility towards whatever lies outside the realm of what one regards as sacred. The rest of the world is "pagan" to these committed eyes. The secular attitude revolts against these assumptions of religion. It would prefer to "belong to the world and its affairs as distinguished from the church and religion." 16274

As for the other meaning of the word "secularization", it can suggest that there is no longer a thirst for any sort of *ek stasis*. This borders on the other central meaning that we have noted: "Of or belonging to the present or visible world, as distinguished from the eternal or spiritual world".

An interesting fact stands out in this brief review of the semantic history of the word "secular". Emerging from its ecclesiastical context in Middle English, the word took over the meaning "non-religious", "non-sacred", at the time of the renaissance and the reformation, even as early as Wyclif. Intellectual and aesthetic activities were gradually liberated from the early domination by religion and one could speak of secular music, architecture, other arts, secular plays, and secular education. This was further emphasized by the liberal-democratic tradition of the nineteenth century. The meaning, "of or belonging to the present or visible world as distinguished from the eternal or spiritual world", assumed prominence about the middle of the nineteenth century when the social and the materialistic philosophies sprang up from a scientifically industrial setting. They distrusted the metaphysics, not only of religion, but of mysticism and endeavoured to promote a vision based entirely on the senses, the intellect and common human emotions. The idealistic thought-movements of the twentieth century are endeavouring to orient the word "secularization" in a third direction: "The diffusion of the quest for ecstasy or for the holy beyond the normal precincts of the sacred or the religious and into the region of the most ordinary experience of life, with a metaphysical structure which varies from one school to another." We may now examine what significance these three meanings have in the context of modern Indian society.

The first meaning of the word "secular" is: "belonging to the world and its affairs as distinguished from religion and the church". The secular is the non-religious or the non-sacred. We have already seen how education, literature, and the fine arts gradually became secularized in Great Britain during the last few centuries. The word "secularization" denotes institutional autonomy. Under the impact of modernization or technological advance, segments of the social structure liberate themselves from the domination of religion. Our economic and political systems seek justification entirely in terms of their own functional logic. The individual does not any longer seek an ultimate meaning in his public roles and functions. This institutional phenomenon leaves individuals free to turn towards the private sphere of family life and introspection in their quest for ultimate meanings and norms. This gradual differentiation between the secular and the private or the religious aspect has become the leading feature of all advanced countries in the world. This is what Maulana Abul Kalam Azad also implied when in his

Presidential address to the Congress in 1940 he remarked:

> The joint wealth is the heritage of our common nationality
> and we do not want to leave it and go back to the times when
> this joint life had not begun. If there are any Hindus
> amongst us who desire to bring back the Hindu life of a
> thousand years ago and more, they dream, and such dreams
> are vain fantasies. So also if there are any Muslims who
> wish to revive their past civilization and culture which they
> brought a thousand years ago from Iran and Central Asia,
> they dream also and the sooner they wake up the better.
> These are unnatural fancies which cannot take root in the
> soil of reality. I am one of those who believe that revival
> may be a necessity in a religion, but in social matters, it is a
> denial of progress.

One cannot say that the state in Great Britain is secular
as it is in the USA or India. But there is probably more of
secularization in British society than we have yet been able to
achieve in India. The domination of public life by considerations of caste, creed, or religion has to go, if we have to build
up a society of enlightened individuals. All citizens have to
be equal before the law, not merely in theory but in actual
practice. All public institutions and posts will be open to
deserving individuals irrespective of the distinction of caste,
community, or creed. No communal colleges, schools, or
hostels will be maintained at the expense of the state. At the
same time, state aid will be available for the uplift of the Schedul-
ed Castes and Tribes, and other backward sections of the
society. Culture will have to be differentiated from religion
as education and the fine arts have been differentiated from it
during the last century and a half. The common Indian heritage should be the common and proud possession of all, what-

ever the community to which they belong. But the great historical personages and their achievements, the monuments of art and architecture, the beauty of the Gita and the Quran as literary classics, the beauty even of Hindu mythology and legend quite apart from religious belief has to be brought home to students in all our universities through a course in composite Indian culture, if they are to develop a love for their common heritage.

But the question arises: Will this concept of secularization suffice for ennobling the lives of our people? The third meaning: "The diffusion of the quest for ecstasy beyond the precincts of the sacred or the religious", is extremely relevant. It would not be correct to assume that a non-religious or non-sacred life is all that is necessary for ensuring national progress. On the other hand, the fact that something more is needed than the functional logic of primary institutions is borne out by the fact that the quest for ecstasy in a technological society like the USA also assumes several forms. Churches proliferate, astrology and psychic research grasp the popular imagination and the search for ecstasy finds escape in drugs.

The Indian Constitution has carefully avoided the use of the word "secular" in any context. But it has given a charter of freedom to every individual to profess any faith, ancient or modern, that he fancies. It does so in these memorable words: "Subject to public order, morality and health and to the other provisions of this part, all persons are equally entitled to freedom of conscience and the right freely to profess, practise and propagate religion."

The Indian State is not antagonistic to any religion, nor does it adopt any one of them as its own. It stands for liberty of conscience and tolerance in the largest sense of the word. At the same time, the Indian Constitution is steeped in the secular spirit. This is seen in the twenty-fifth chapter on fundamental rights and in the autonomy of logical functioning that it has guaranteed to all political and economic organizations. It has to be brought home to the traditionalist that tolerance for the other man's faith is the basic condition for living in a multi-religious society. As Gandhiji said: "I regard the great faiths of the world as so many branches of a tree, each distinct from the other though having the same source." If the traditionalist does not realize this, he may come under the spell of non-secular forces.

Tolerance and coexistence are essential. But the secularization of the inner life also has another meaning. It concerns itself more with psychology than with religion. The problem is that of integrating and controlling one's own faculties and being in tune with oneself and with reality. But since the traditional complex of "ultimate" meanings and norms is no longer disseminated and affirmed by the primary institutions, the main job has to be done either by the individual himself or by educational institutions. The pace for this kind of psychological evolution and fulfilment has been set by mystics and seers. They showed how the spiritual life can be separate from institutional religion, by concentrating on the essential significance of symbols and rituals and the meaning that they have for the pilgrim of eternity. It is also possible to interpret each religion in a liberal and personal way and be a good Christian without going to church or a good Hindu without visiting a shrine. The autonomy of this private sphere of sanctity has also to be promoted in each individual along with "the legitimation of economic or political systems." If the individual is not enabled to cultivate this "solitude" or sanctity in the private sphere in the midst of the multitude, if his quest for ecstasy cannot proceed freely and spontaneously, he is bound to be a problem in his approach as a citizen to the primary institutions themselves. In our anxiety to secularize education we have not been mindful of this tremendous responsibility which is as important as the emancipation of our primary institutions from the domination of religion.

Then there is the last meaning: "Of or belonging to the present or visible world as distinguished from the eternal or spiritual world." A modern philosophy like communism has turned into a religion by itself in its attempt to get away from religion and all that it implies. A secular state may guarantee tolerance and freedom of conscience, if it wants to, as the Republic of India does. But a secular state may go further and make a secular philosophy its official philosophy. It may also wish to promote the existence of a secular society. Bigotry and fanaticism, which disfigured life in the middle ages, leading to religious wars and feuds because the followers of one religion or sect thought their own to be superior to the other, is on the wane in the modern world. The maximum of human liberty prospers in a state which guarantees freedom of faith and the autonomy of primary institutions. A private form of faith deserves to have as much autonomy as a private form of worship. But the moment it tries to interfere with the freedom of individuals and their liberty of conscience, we begin to be confronted by a dogmatic creed which becomes as intolerant as any theological system.

The supreme need of the hour seems to be the promotion and nationwide multiplication of the secular citizen and the integrated Indian. He will be secular in the sense that he does not allow his religion and world view to intrude upon others or on the working of primary institutions. He will be secular also in the sense that he does not abandon the quest for esctasy and for ultimate meanings but pursues it either in the privacy of his own soul, or in the traditional way, without offending other traditions. Even if he subscribes to one of those modern philosophies, which take their stand on matter rather than spirit, he will not commit the ancient or medieval error of coercing others to accept his philosophy. It is in the universal affirmation and diffusion of such an attitude that the perfect fulfilment of Indian nationhood lies.

9

*Indian Literature
as an Expression
of Indian Culture*

Speaking of Indian literature, one has to think of European literature as a parallel rather than of English, French, or German literature. For we are dealing here with a literature some of whose constituents, like Tamil or Kannada literature, go back to the beginnings of the Christian era. Indeed, Tamil dates back earlier than the Christian era itself. The prakrits prevailed over Sanskrit eventually owing to the impetus given to them by the Buddha and Mahavira and they became the progenitors of many of the modern Indian languages which can claim a literary ancestry more than a thousand years old. Sanskrit, Persian, Arabic, and English during the period of the British connection became the seminal languages that influenced the regional literatures in varying degrees. These were to the regional literatures what Greek and Latin have been to European literature. All modern Indian languages are national languages. But they are the vehicles of only one literature—the national literature of India. Sanskrit, Persian, and English have also been the official languages of India during their own periods and Indian literature was and is being transmitted through these languages too.

Though Indian literature can be compared only to European literature because of its composite character, it can, in another sense, be compared to any individual component of it. This is so because the Republic of India is one country like the United Kingdom, France, Germany, or the USA. It is composite and unitive at the same time, like Russia. It is true that the Indian literature that came after the European Renaissance is not so well developed as European literature, because the Middle Ages lingered on in India almost till the beginning of the nineteenth century. But the modern Indian languages have been the vehicles of a pre-Renaissance literature that is as full of vitality as the literature of that period in any other country.

The concept of a national literature is part of current critical parlance and so are the concepts of comparative and world literature. I shall concentrate here on the Indianness of Indian literature or the characteristics of Indian literature as the literature of the Indian people.

We may remember in this connection that certain critical opinions are expressed now and then which point to such distinctive traits. For example, Keats has been described by some critics as a pagan or Greek born out of his time. Many of us are also inclined to think that poets like Keats and Shelley appeal more than other English poets to the Indian mind. There is a certain amount of ethereality and idealism about their poetry which seems to be very much akin to the Indian manner. It should be possible for us to investigate what we, mean when we institute comparisons of this kind.

The Aryan and the Dravidian are the two major races that have contributed greatly to the making of the Indian people. The Semitic and other elements came in later and had their own contribution to make. Indian literature represents the hopes and aspirations of this multi-racial community called the Indian people. Their approach to reality was marked by certain distinctive attitudes. The early Indian people generally believed in the primacy of spirit as, indeed, many Indians do even today. They affirmed the reconciliation of matter and spirit, earth, the mother, and heaven, the father, as Vivekananda, Gandhiji and Sri Aurobindo have done in modern times. They accepted life in its totality, the temporal and the eternal, the physical and the metaphysical, and sought to include them in a luminous and harmonious synthesis. This, at least, is what the Vedas and the Upanishads stand for. One sees this in the literature and art of the Mauryan and Gupta periods, in the literature that included Patanjali and Vatasyayana. They believed in reincarnation and metemsychosis, a belief that influenced the writings of Roman story-tellers like Ovid. Their mythopoeic imagination was responsible for glorious myths like the churning of the ocean and the love of Shiva and Parvati, Upanishadic parables like those of Satyakama and Nachiketas and early legends like those of Savitri and Damayanti. Heroic characters like Ravana might border on fantasy. But personages like Rama and Sita, Laxmana, Arjun and Draupadi were cast in an archetypal heroic mould that nothing could surpass. There were lovely symbols, *Agni* or fire, symbolizing upward human aspiration, *Usha*, spiritual dawn and the dawn of day, and the Upanishadic pair of birds one of which is a detached spectator and the other an active participant in the cosmic scene. All these are only a fraction of the rich legacy that the Aryo-Dravidian imagination conferred on mankind through a distinctive literature.

The doctrine of *Maya* or illusion, propounded by Shankara and later emphasized in various directions, led to the general impression that prevails outside India, suggesting that the Indian outlook on life is otherworldly. *Mayavad* might have had some such effect on some sections of people in India during the Middle Ages. But this is not Indian philosophy as it can be gleaned from the Vedas and the Upanishads.

The commingling of Semitic and other races with the Aryo-

Dravidian people at a later date produced a new language and a new literature: Urdu and the mystical treatises written by the medieval Sufi saints. The British or the European impact brought in a number of new developments in the physical and social sciences of India and new forces and factors like democracy, social justice, and technology. These affected the literature produced in all the Indian languages and the British inspact was responsible for a new Indian literature, Indo-Anglian literature.

The distinctiveness of the Indian setting left its own impress on Indian literature. If Venus is the morning and evening star in European poetry and is frequently written about, Indian poetry speaks of the Pleiades known as the Saptarshi Mandala. The Pleiades caught the imagination of the early Indian poets and a newly married Hindu couple on their wedding night are expected to see the Arundhati star in that constellation. Shelley describes the moon as "the orbed maiden with white fire laden". The moon struck the European imagination as a lady. But Indian poetry speaks of the moon in the masculine with the star called *Rohini* as his consort. Speaking of birds, it is not the albatross, the nightingale, or the *bulbul* that early Indian poets spoke of. These came later. Their lyric raptures are aroused by the kokil, the eagle, the peacock, and the swan. The swan or *hamsa* becomes famous in Indian literature as the symbol of the soul. For example, Sri Rama Krishna was known as "Paramahamsa", the surpassing or transendental self. The eagle was supposed to carry god Vishnu on its back. Similarly, the *airavat* or white elephant is Indra's favourite, and *vrishabha* or the ox is the favourite animal of Shiva. The cow was regarded sacred by the Hindus and the lamb joined it in its sacredness when Christianity came to India. As for trees, it is the *aswatha,* the mango, the deodar, and the sandal-wood tree that are famous in early Indian poetry. The parijat tree and the tulsi plant also developed their own legendary associations. The cheenar was introduced by the Mughals and the maple, the poplar and the oak came in with the British. The lotus, the *champak* and the jasmine were flowers loved by early Indian poets. The rose came in with Muslim rulers and the pansy, the daffodil, the poppy and other flowers when the British had settled down to rule India. The Himalayas have moved Indian poets to raptures and Kalidasa has spoken of the Himalayan range as the measuring rod of the earth. The Himalayan and Dandakaranya forests have rich legendary association in Indian poetry. It was the Mughals who made gardens like those in Kashmir, the haunt and theme of poets. The beauty of summer hill-stations entered Indian literature only after the advent of the British. The summer heat of tropical plains in India and the cycle of seasons have been described beautifully by Kalidasa and other poets.

The Indian poets also described gloriously ancient cities like Pataliputra, Ujjain, and Madura and the late medieval cities like Vijayanagara, Delhi, and Jaipur. Cities like Bombay and Chandigarh are described in modern Indian writings.

The great Indian rivers like the Ganges, the Jamuna, and the Kaveri have been celebrated by poets in moving poetry. The Ganga is, above all, the sacred river par excellence with many myths woven around it. It has its counterpart in the Milky Way and the subterranean river in the underworld of Hindu mythology. Indian poetry from very early times to Raja Rao's *The Serpant and the Rope* has been full of it and even fastidious poets like T.S. Eliot have invoked it effectively in English poetry.

One has also to remember in this connection the new environment created by industrialization. Factories of various kinds, railway trains, ships, and aeroplanes are as much a part of the Indian scene today as of the European. Space exploration is as yet an American or Russian venture. But the world is fast becoming one in these matters and modern Indian writers have not hesitated to exploit this fact for their lyric effusion and imagery.

Human society is as much a part of the environment of poets as nature is. The Indian writer has responded to the changing panorama of human society from very early days. The Vedas contain a mention of fierce tribal wars. Valmiki and Vyasa have made the heroic age in India famous throughout the world by their great epics. The Mauryan, Gupta, and Harsha periods have left their mark over Sanskrit poetry, drama, and prose. This tradition of mirroring the political and social history of the times was taken up later by poets in the regional languages. The palace intrigues in the court of Kashmir kings have been presented in historical perspective by Kalhana in Sanskrit and there are many pictures of the life in feudal Indian society by medieval writers in various Indian languages. New movements like democracy, nationalism, humanism, and socialism have been changing Indian society. Modern poetry, drama, and fiction give powerful pictures of these transitions. From the agricultural society of early times, as reflected in the Vedas, to the highly sophisticated atmosphere in a machine tools factory, Indian literature has held up the mirror to Indian society in all its changing contours and patterns. For example, when the Europeans appeared on the Indian scene in their outlandish dress, Indian poets were not slow in registering their arrival. They spoke of strangers who wore "bodices" for their feet. This was how the socks that Europeans wore struck them.

Indian literature has thus been the mirror held up faithfully to the life of the Indian people with their diverse racial affinities, religions and manners. There are numerous collections of satirical stories centring around rulers, religious men, merchants, soldiers, and the like. Collections of profane stories like Boccaccio's De Cameron are not wanting. Indeed, the tradition of such stories might as well be regarded as having started very early in India, and then proceeded towards Europe. Historic moments in the life of the people have been presented with all their tragedy, pathos, and grandeur from time to time. The historic encounters of Alexandar and Porus, Prithvi Raj and Mahmud Ghuri, Babar and Rana Sangram and of Ram Raya of Vijayanagar and the confederecy of the southern Muslim kingdoms have haunted the Indian imagination and have been presented in drama, fiction, and verse. Crucial moments in the history of the nation, like the Dandi March of Gandhiji which shook the very foundations of the British Empire and the tragic partition of India, have been sung about by distinguished poets as well as folk balladists.

I have spoken so far of the characteristic imagination of Indian people and of the panoramic setting in the midst of which they lived and wrote. But, after all, the Indianness of Indian literature springs from the genius of Indian writers themselves. Writers are the nerve-centres of a people's culture and the whole of it speaks through its writers, vivified by racial imagination and memory, and drawing upon its natural and social environment for themes and imagery. Vedic sages like Vishwamitra and Deerghatamas, the Upanishadic seers, epic poets like Valmiki and Vaysa, prophets like the Buddha and Mahavira, people's poets like Kabir, Tulsidas, Sarvajna and Vemana, and modern writers like Ghalib, Tagore, Sri Aurobindo, Prem Chand, and K.M. Munshi have to be studied intensively to grasp the Indianness of Indian literature. Persons belonging to different faiths like the Rev. Vaman Tilak, the Marathi Christian poet, and Sarif Sahib, the Kannada Muslim poet, have contributed to the variety and richness of this literature.

Indian literature, as has been said, is one though written in many languages. It acquired two more tongues during the medieval and modern periods: Urdu and English. It presents a fascinating picture of the pageantry of Indian life and its panoramic evolution down the ages. The traditions of the early Indian period flow along with other traditions when the stream of Indian life broadens out into a greater and greater expanse, fed by other tributaries. As Indian literature stands today, it presents all those attitudes to life that characterize the Western poet and man of letters. If one were to point out a few distinctive features of Indian literature, one would be tempted to say that the best of it gives the quintessence of a living culture that is unique and more than three thousands years old. Secondly, representing as it does a confluence of diverse races and religions, it presents at its best, a picture of tolerance and understanding, a living and creative synthesis which it would be hard to match elsewhere. This approach has its modern exponents in men of genius like Tagore, Sri Aurobindo, and Gandhiji. Thirdly, there is the background, to a good part of this literary activity, of a psychology, a metaphysics, an aesthetics, a metrics, a linguistics, and a theory of literature that is a living and unique tradition, going back to the early days of Indian civilization. A literature has finally to be judged both by the complexity and variety of the experience which it communicates and the sense of inclusive unity which it imparts. Modern European literature has, probably, more of this complexity than Indian literature. But the sense of inclusive unity that pervades Indian literature is probably unparalleled. It has been generally acknowledged that Indian civilization is one of the major civilizations of the world. Indian literature, which has mirrored its fortunes faithfully down the centuries, is naturally entitled to a similar claim.

II

All writers belong to the republic of letters, whatever their nationality. A creative writer—be he a poet, dramatist, novelist, or anything else—is one who communicates experiences or states of consciousness which are valuable for their own sake. For this reason, the republic of letters extends backwards and forward in time and everywhere in space. To it belong Valmiki and Homer, Shakespeare and Goethe, Tagore and T.S. Eliot.

How can one define the contemporary Indian writer? It is true that each writer carries with him the climate of the part of the republic to which he belongs. In that sense, a contemporary Indian writer is one whose sensibility is aglow from the inside with the four-fold paradox that India is today. His ideological angle may be his own. It is bound to be conditioned by his upbringing and his temperamental choice. But for him to be truly Indian, and in the contemporary sense, his sensibility must have been stirred by as many facets of this four-fold paradox as possible. The more facets his consciousness is able to touch, the more comprehensive, artistically speaking, will be his approach. A good deal also depends on the depths which he is able to sound. His perspective may be one of satire, humour, comedy, tragedy, pathos or indignation. The predominance of a particular aesthetic motive or attitude depends upon the direction towards which his genius inclines.

What, then, is the four-fold paradox that is contemporary India? In the first place, India is a country rich in its resources and potentialities but dire in its poverty; great in its cultural heritage but pathetic in the colossal ignorance that enshrouds its people. Neither has it evolved into the technological moon-era like Russia and the USA nor has it developed into an industrial society like the UK, France, or Japan. Science and industry are as yet only a patch on this vast geographical mass of medieval and agricultural pursuits. The unemployment in our country is incredible, staggering in its figures; and student unrest proceeds from causes which are totally different from those in the developed countries. Our conditions may resemble those obtaining in other developing countries. But the scale on which this happens with us is, in every way, colossal. As D.R Bendre said in one of his Kannada lyrics, the voice of the people thunders:

> *We'll bury God under the ground*
> *And visit his tomb on our nightly round.*
> *Stung into madness by death-dearth,*
> *We'll make a morsel of this earth!*

Secondly, we live in a country which believes in unity in diversity but is actually diverse in its perversity. We have not yet been freed from the colonial yoke in many departments of life. A great social upsurge is afoot; our tribals, Harijans, backward classes, and first generation learners are impatient over the time-lags caused by history and are determined to come into their own, whatever flutter that may cause in shelterd dove-cotes. There is the upheaval of classes in Indian society: the feudalism that is fading; the upper middle class that consists of the new and uncultured rich, political middlemen and un-scrupulous businessmen; the middle class that is suffering impatiently, breaking up or taking to new professions; and the proletariat that is strident in its speech and action. The various religious communities still tend to live in separate pockets though in one and the same society. Castes and creeds still dominate the civic and political life. Our cities are expanding at an ungainly rate and the villages are getting depleted of their population or faction-ridden because of elections. Linguism stalks abroad and regionalism lifts its ugly head in river-water disputes and border-disputes between one State and the other.

115

Thirdly, India, which is the biggest democracy in the world and has stood its ground, as has been proved abundantly in the recent elections to Parliament, is yet the least literate among the democracies of the world. Democracy as a way of life has yet to strike root. No doubt there has been a galaxy of great men in recent years. But how do a few tall pines and oaks count in a forest of furze and briar? It is the dumb millions that matter and they are inarticulate, if not ineffective, because of our power-seekers and the infiltration of politics into all walks of life. China, with its proletarian dictatorship, has whipped up a cultural revolution. We have embarked on a much greater experiment: the democratization of the whole of Indian society. And, naturally, this takes time.

Lastly, we are the heirs of one of the greatest cultures—the oldest living culture in the world. And yet we are busy learning our first elementary lessons in science, technology, and secularism from the West. There is a great deal of interest abroad in the Indian heritage. It will continue to live in many museums and libraries even if we imagine that it will be supplanted in India. But the exact balance between the East and West has yet to be struck by singling out those factors which make for national acceptance, unlike Japan where this has been achieved in some measure. The result is that this clash of cultures has given rise in India to ideologies that oscillate all the way from mysticism to Maoism. We are living in a welter of ideologies.

This is the four-fold paradox of contemporary India, tragic and comic, moving us now to tears and now to side-splitting laughter. If we imagine an Indian writer with an olympian vision and a multi-dimensional genius, one whose soul is more comprehensive than even of Shakespeare, how would he be writing today?

He would describe the sublimity of nature in India—her

116

Himalayan peaks, great historic rivers, rolling plains and picturesque forests, and the pageantry that the cycle of seasons projects against this background from time to time. Contrasting with this, he would paint grim pictures of the poverty and ignorance that enchain a great people, the squalor and misery that is India. He would move his readers to infinite pity and indignation, like a socialist, Marxist or Maoist. He would make a passionate plea for action, instantaneous action to wipe out these evils and usher in a new economic order.

Changing his key, in another mood, he would harp, in an impassioned strain, on the need for reason and sanity, for secular integration. He would give fascinating pictures of tribal life, sing to folk tunes like Burns, describe the tensions suffered by first generation learners, the conflict between Brahmin and neo-Buddhist, analyze Hindu-Muslim riots, unveil the agony of the dying feudal and middle class that is living and partly living, pull the legs of politicians and the new rich, paint the ghastly life of cities where necessity is supreme and the broken life of the countryside which was a paradise of peace some decades ago, lay bare the edge of rivalry between state and state or take a last lingering look at colonialism and the white sahib of yesterday.

In a graver and more devastating mood, the olympian writer would turn his gaze full on the political life in the country and speak of the democracy that is yet to come of age in the biggest democracy of the world. He would strike an ethical note and discourse on the collapse of moral values and the climate of corruption and jobbery. He would caricature ministers and parliamentarians, defectors and presidents of municipalities, district local boards and panchayats. He would, as T.P. Kailasam did, speak of home rule in a home where there is only one master and that is the mistress and the rule that no two municipal councillors should live in the same

117

street so that there will be as many streets lit municipally as there are councillors.   He would show the impact of great men and women of the Indian Renaissance in his novels and plays. He would sing the chorus of the unemployed, unemployable millions and expose the tragedy of our education—the circus of Saraswati crowded with memorizing animals and mummies. He would dwell on the conflict of generations and the breath-taking fun of fast-changing fashions.

In a more serene moment, the Indian writer with an olympian vision would contemplate the tragi-comic panorama that is India—the glory, jest, and riddle of the world. He would escape into a world of fantasy and dream, dig up the past in historical romances, turn pessimist, optimist, cynic, surrealist or existentialist and gambol in the theatre of the Absurd. Or he would build up a new theory of human evolution and integral vision, announcing the advent of the superman and the millennium.   He would explore his own religious tradition and rebel against it even while hugging it.

As for form, the contemporary Indian writer experiments with a number of diseases, mannerisms and modes of expression. He has a touch of literary diarrhoea like the romantic or literary constipation like the modernist.   Or he takes up a classical literary form like the epic and hammers it into a new shape like Sri Aurobindo.   He can be obsessed with folk tunes or folk art-forms.   He can float on the stream of consciousness or forge an anti-novel out of sheer cussedness.   He can afford to be amorphous or revel in the condition of literary protoplasm.

This, then, is the Indian writer who holds the literary fort, and conditions the literary scene today.   Imagine the magic mirror of this olympion vision splintered into a million frag-ments and that will give a good idea of the contemporary republic of letters in India.   The magic consists in the smooth-ening of contours in the mirror and in the attempt to hint at solutions. As Indian democracy slowly takes shape, the writer may deal with more radiant themes, groping his way towards national art-forms.

But this does not mean that there is no glory in his vision of the four-fold paradox. Even as he writes, he is an active participant in a great aesthetic adventure, one of untold significance for the future of the human race. For it is here, on Indian soil, that the pattern of the world culture of tomorrow is on the anvil for being fashioned in all its unity and complexity.

10

Culture's Coming of Age

Man looks before and after and strives hard to pave the way for his own eventual perfection. A few gifted thinkers in every generation have thought and written about the future of humanity. The second coming of Christ, the presence of the Buddha in the earth atmosphere until the last human soul is freed from bondage and ignorance, the Avatar, the descent of supermind to speed up the evolution of man into superman—this is how our seers and sages have responded to the challenge of time and embodied their hopes and visions, their faith in words and images of enduring loveliness.

A writer has classified into three groups the writers who have imagined their own utopias. One of these consists of "deteriorationists". They think that, with constantly deteriorating conditions, the doom is well within sight. In a sermon that he delivered in 999 A.D., Wulfstan, an English clergyman and prose writer, prophesied that the world would come to an end in 1000 A.D. But the year was as normal or abnormal as any other. Today again we have similar prophets of doom who predict the same calamity for the year 2000 A.D. Some people see the end of the world in the end of a millennium.

Thomas Hardy, in one of his poems, spoke of:

Godhead dying downwards,
Brain and eye now gone.

But he wrote hopefully of the cuckoo that sang to him on the eve of the last day of the year 1900 A.D. It gave him a message of hope:

> *Some blessed hope whereof he knew*
> *And I was unaware.*

But pessimists can also be incurable, like Toobad in T.L. Peacock's philosophic novel, *Nightmare Abbey*.

A second group consists of status quoites. They believe that the cosmic pattern is set once for all and that no change is envisaged or possible. There may be infinite repetition within the cosmic framework, but each event is unique. Heraclitus, the Greek philosopher, believed that the universe was in an eternal flux. John Donne, the metaphysical poet who echoed him, said that although the river may be the same, yesterday's waters and today's are not the same. Kapila, the founder of the Sankhya school of philosophy, posited the dual reality of *Prakriti* or Nature and *Purusha* or Being implying that this world play, this cosmic game, would proceed endlessly in this manner through the interaction of *Prakriti* and *Purusha*. Zoroaster, the prophet of Iran, assumed that the two "principles of evil and good" are eternally in conflict with each other and that history is but the record of their interaction and conflict through the ages. Camus even infused an element of the Absurd into this status quoism by comparing all human activity to the labours of Sisyphus. Just as the pessimist forgets that there is a silver lining to every cloud, the status quoite seems to overlook the fact that there is an emergent purpose in evolution and that we cannot draw a line and say that man is the last word in creation. It may be that an eternal flux is the only truth, if man continues to be what he is. But it would be a different thing if, at a certain stage in this evolution, not reached as yet, man were to be transformed

121

radically and become the heir of other powers and potentialities.

A third group consists of perfectibiliarians or thinkers who believe that perfection is possible, though remote. They differ among themselves as to the means prescribed for attaining perfection. They also have different notions of perfection itself. Some of them champion reason and materialism. Perfection connotes great material prosperity and happiness for these thinkers. In his *New Atlantis*, Bacon imagined a utopian island full of a prosperity of this kind. The learned father in Solomon's House in this island aimed at "the knowledge of causes and of the secret motions of things; and the enlarging of the bounds of human empire to the effect of all things possible." Bacon anticipated in this utopia that there would be airships and ships for going under water. All this has been achieved now and we are yet as far away from perfection and happiness as people were in the days of Bacon and Queen Elizabeth I. But Bacon drops casually a hint which seems to be far more significant than the rest of the picture. The father of Solomon's House has "an aspect as if he pitied men." It is this sense of pity or compassion that is responsible for all advancement of science and altruism. It may even lead us to the heights of peace and tranquillity.

Realism naturally goes with reason and materialism as one of the means that pave the way to perfection. As Macaulay says: "An acre of Middlesex is worth a province in utopia."

Advancing further on the Baconian path, Haldane predicts the cosmic supremacy of mankind. In *A Modern Utopia,* H.G. Wells imagines that man will move towards perfection and attain unalloyed happiness when there is no unemployment, when crime is regarded a disease and the criminal a patient fit to be hospitalized rather than imprisoned and when the world speaks one language, destroying the Tower of Babel for ever, and comes under the sway of one government under the sun.

This line of thinking certainly contains an aspect of truth. It is that reason has been a great boon to mankind and that it can lead man to a continuous and ever-increasing mastery of his environment. Reason should be cultivated, if man is to be happy and prosperous. It is on this gospel of reason that the utopias of the rationalists and materialists are founded.

But there is Plato's *Republic* which directs our gaze to the other side of the medal. Plato insists that man should be good of his kind if he is to be happy. Reason alone cannot make a man happy. It is goodness rather than reason that brings about a state of blessedness or felicity. A philosophic mind, an enthusiasm for ideas, and an eagerness to value the intensity and variety of experience for its own sake are the authentic constituents of a genuine formula for human happiness. As for the economy of the individual and the State, Plato spells out a kind of equality based on primitive communism. Sir Thomas More in his *Utopia* advocates a kind of socialism rooted in agriculture.

The Platonic view finds its near affinity in *News From Nowhere* by William Morris, the Pre-Raphaelite poet. Morris would like to scrap all machinery or, at any rate, have none of it at the expense of spirit. Gott, in his *The New Jerusalem,* projects a theocratic republic. The ethical aspect is somewhat overstressed in this book. No drinks are to be served anywhere in this republic and children cannot marry without the consent of their parents. Unless there is a spontaneous love and regard for the other man, no system can work and bring about the desired result. Even with governments that explicitly recognize the imperative need for equality between man and man, a fully co-operative life in all contexts and at all levels will be possible only on the basis of spontaneous love. The fullness of love unfolds itself when man cultivates his reason as well as his emotions, fellow-feeling as well as eagerness to explore the inner recesses of his own personality. We finally come back to the great quartet of absolutes: love, truth, goodness, and beauty. By beauty is meant the innocence and refinement of emotions as well as the transformation of one's environment by an intensive cultivation and application of the fine arts so that refined emotions are naturally evoked by the atmosphere in which one lives and moves.

It is easy to make fun of the utopias imagined by these great writers. The guardians of Plato's *Republic* have been dubbed as philosophic country squires. The Bensalemites of Bacon are said to resemble the duller professors. The best that certain critics are inclined to say about More's utopians is that they are, at most, a decent sort of people. The republic which Shelley conceived and presented in *The Revolt of Islam* is also said to be colourless, for the lovers in that romantic epic do nothing but eat vegetables and read Plato. We are told that the Samurai of H.G. Wells have only a higher abdominal development and that the neurotics in Bernard Shaw's *Back to Methuselah* only excite pity. Orwell's prophecies are full of relentless cynicism and pessimism.

Some kind of simplification, undoubtedly, take place when a writer wants to emphasize one or the other aspect of the human personality. We are reminded of Shakespeare's parody of Montaigne's utopia when Gonzalo, stranded with the royal party on the celebrated island in *The Tempest,* sets forth his idea of a commonwealth.

So long as the average man remains a prey to jealousy, greed and other weaknesses of the flesh, a total regeneration of humanity is a far cry. But the cultural conquests of man have to be measured by what the daring few have achieved. The universal diffusion of culture as such can be assessed only by ascertaining how far it has left an impact on the generality of mankind. One may remember, in this connection, Sri Aurobindo's concept of the superman. Sri Aurobindo's superman moves in a direction totally different from Nietzshe's. He grows into a centre of power—the fifth absolute—but not the power of the glorified vital, of brute force, whose votary Nietzsche's superman is. Nietzsche sowed the wind and reaped the whirlwind called Hitler. The power that Sri Aurobindo's superman has is the power of spirit.

In his *Life Divine,* Sri Aurobindo speaks of the integral transformation towards which humanity has to evolve. Supermind or Truth-Consciousness, the *Rit Chit*, is the apex of the evolutionary urge that has now reached the mental principle. It has to go further and the evolution will continue till the emergence of a divine life on earth. Gnostic beings will first gravitate towards each other on earth and a gnostic brotherhood will be formed even in the midst of ignorance. Sri Aurobindo says:

The influence of the supramental principle on earth would fall upon the life of the ignorance and impose harmony on it within its limits. It is conceivable that the gnostic life would be separate, but it would surely admit within its borders as much of human life as was turned towards spirituality and in progress towards the heights; the rest might organise itself mainly on the mental principle and on the old foundations, but, helped and influenced by a recognisable greater knowledge, it would be likely to do so on lines of a complete harmonisation of which the human collectivity is not yet capable. Here also, however, the mind can only forecast probabilities and possibilities; the superamental principle in Supernature would itself determine according to the truth of things the balance of a new world-order.

The Mother, who is working for Sri Aurobindo's ideals in the Ashram at Pondicherry, has conceived and launched a project known as *Auroville* which was supported unanimously by UNESCO at its General Conference, held in Paris in 1968, under Resolution 4:

Noting that the foundation stone of Auroville has been laid on 28 February 1968 and that the youth of many nations participated in this solemn ceremony symbolizing the coming together of nations in a spirit of human unity.

Confident that Auroville with its many interrelated sub-projects will add a new dimension to UNESCO's activities for the promotion of international co-operation and understanding and appreciation of cultural and human values.

Invites Member States and international non-governmental organizations to participate in the development of Auroville as an international cultural township designed to bring together the values of different cultures and civilisations in a harmonious environment with integrated living standards which correspond to man's physical and spiritual needs.

The Mother had written beautifully about Auroville as a "dream" before all these developments had taken place:

There should be somewhere upon earth a place that no nation could claim as its sole property, a place where all human beings of goodwill, sincere in their aspiration, could live freely as citizens of the world, obeying one single authority, that of the supreme truth, a place of peace, concord, harmony, where all the fighting instincts of man would be used exclusively to conquer the causes of his sufferings and miseries, to surmount his weakness and ignorance, to triumph over his limitations and incapacities; a place where the needs of the spirit and the care for progress would get precedence over the satisfaction of desires and passions, the seeking for material pleasures and enjoyment. In this place, children would be able to grow and develop integrally without losing contact with their soul. Education would be given not with a view to passing examinations and getting certificates and posts but for enriching the existing faculties and bringing forth new ones. In this place titles and positions would be supplanted by opportunities to serve and organise. The needs of the body will be provided for equally in the case of each and every one. In the general organisation, intellectual, moral and spiritual superiority will find expression not in the enhancement of the pleasures and powers of life but in the increase of duties and responsibilities. Artistic beauty in all forms—painting, sculpture, music, literature, etc.—will be available equally to all, the opportunity to share in the joys they give being limited solely by each one's capacities and not by social or financial position. For in this ideal place money would be no more the sovereign lord. Individual value would have a greater importance than the value due to material wealth and social position. Work would not be there as the means for gaining one's livelihood, it would be the means whereby to express oneself, develop one's capacities and possibilities, while doing at the same time service to the whole group, which on its side would provide for each one's subsistence and for the field of his work. In brief, it would be a place where the relations among human beings, usually based upon competition and strife, would be replaced by relations of emulation for doing better, for collaboration, relations of real brotherhood.

The earth is certainly not ready to realize such an ideal, for mankind does not yet possess the necessary knowledge to understand and accept it nor the indispensable conscious force to execute it. That is why I call it a dream.

Yet this dream is on the way of becoming a reality. That is exactly what we are seeking to do at the Ashram of Sri Aurobindo on a small scale, in proportion to our modest means. The achievement is indeed far from being perfect but it is progressive; little by little we advance towards our goal, which, we hope, one day we shall be able to hold before the world as a practical and effective means of coming out of the present chaos in order to be born into a more true, more harmonious new life.

As work progressed on Auroville, she gave the Auroville charter on 28 February 1968.

(1) Auroville belongs to nobody in particular. Auroville belongs to humanity as a whole. But to live in Auroville one must be a willing servitor of the Divine Consciousness.

(2) Auroville will be the place of an unending education, of constant progress and a youth that never ages.

(3) Auroville wants to be the bridge between the past and the future. Taking advantage of all discoveries from without and from within Auroville will boldly spring towards future realizations.

(4) Auroville will be a site of material and spiritual researches for a living embodiment of an actual Human Unity.

This is a practical project which is being implemented, supported by the power of spirit. It promises to be one of the most significant projects of this country.

On the whole, one can say that the culture of the world tomorrow is bound to move in a fourfold direction. Civilization tomorrow is going to be an electronic civilization. Even the latest gifts of science will have to penetrate every nook and cornor of the earth and be harnessed to the service of every portion of mankind, be it white, black, red, brown or yellow. This is inescapable, for knowledge can never continue to be a hidden treasure for a long time. Again, civilization is going to be a global, a planetary civilization. Science has knit the world together and it may soon make even interplanetary life a practical possibility. No more will there be any groups of human beings left to struggle and linger in a primitive milieu outside the pale of civilization. Thirdly, civilization is going to be a *conscious* process, both internally and externally. Knowledge and wisdom will grow hand in hand and be the common property of mankind. The experience that human beings have gained of the interior of the human personality as well as of the world outside will be shared by all and each human being will evolve consciously and integrally towards his goal. Lastly, civilization will be unitive. Human beings will be held together by the bonds of love and realize their essential unity in the light of the Supreme whose children they are. Wealth, desire, duty, and illumination are the four supreme values. Civilization is going to fulfill itself by making them the warp and woof of the individual as well as the collective, life.

This may sound facile, facetious, or sentimental. But the inexorable logic of circumstance is ready at hand to enforce it here and now. Man has either to tread this path or sing the hymn of hate and be involved in a universal destruction. The advanced nations of the world can no longer hope to buy peace and prosperity by patronizing underdeveloped countries and extending to them a condescending hand. Inequalities have to be made up and gaps bridged without any fuss, for there is no hope for man unless he moves unitedly in the great task of reforming himself and the world around him.

It is in this fourfold consummation, made possible by the cultivation of the four absolutes I spoke of, that the future of the world lies.

Appendix

A Note on Kroeber's Views
on the Nature of Culture

The anthropologist today claims that the study of culture is his special field. Kroeber, regarded as the doyen of anthropologists, suggests that civilization means "a body or stream of products of mental exercise".[1] He again refers to it as "the historically differentiated and variable mass of customary ways of functioning of human societies."[2] In another context he says that in addition to content, channelled or selected forms, norms and values, culture also includes human behaviour, for what also matters is the way forms and patterns of culture work or function as a group of human beings lives under them. He makes no distinction between culture and civilization. The word "culture" is used as the customary term applicable alike to high or low products of societies. "Civilization" is used as the term for the larger and richer cultures, carrying an overtone of high development of a society.

This can be a working definition for our purposes. It is a far cry from Matthew Arnold's description of culture as a passion for perfection. We shall presently see that cultivation and refinement are only a part of what the anthropologist tends to regard as culture.

The word "culture" itself is a mid-19th century German word used in the sense anthropologists are using it today. In the sense of "becoming more cultured", the German word goes back to the end of the 18th century.

A few anthropologists like Weber tend to distinguish between culture and civilization in a special way. In Weber's view, civilization corresponds with science and technology; culture with philosophy, religion, and the arts. Culture is restricted to philosophy, religion and art, because the arts have always to begin all over again. They progress independently and in different directions. Civilizational culture is objective whereas cultural culture is subjective. Another

[1] *The Nature of Culture*, p. 40.
[2] *Ibid.*, p. 157.

distinguished anthropologist, MacIver, has even said that civilization connotes a set of means and culture a set of ends.

Kroeber enumerates the qualities of culture as follows:

(1) It is transmitted and continued not by the genetic mechanism of heredity but by inter-conditioning of zygotes.

(2) Whatever its origins in or through individuals, culture quickly tends to become suprapersonal and anonymous and belongs to a whole community of people.

(3) It falls into patterns or regularities of form and style and significance so that one national culture stands off distinctly from the other.

(4) It embodies values which may be formulated as mores or folkways by the society carrying the culture. It is in its affect-laden idea system that the core of a culture lies. It is an objectively expressed freedom of subjective values and this is called its ethos, genius or master-pattern.

We may also try to define the contents of culture or civilization. There are four kinds of phenomena which are called real: of matter and force or the inorganic; of life or the directly organic or vital; of consciousness or the mentally organic or psychic; and lastly of social life or culture which may be referred to as the civilizational or superorganic or superpsychic. Four kinds of sciences deal with these phenomena: the physical and chemical in the realm of the inorganic, the biological in the domain of the organic, the psychological concerned with the psychic aspects of the organic or the mental, and the social sciences operating with superorganic phenomena.

The data of these four levels can be either reviewed as they are depicted and their qualitative values traced or we can pass through them to the processes involved, directing our enquiry into the mechanisms themselves. The functional-social approach is microscopic, concerned with causes and effects and with the practical. The historical-cultural approach is macroscopic or telescopic and is oriented towards the interrelations and significances of the products of culture. The four levels of phenomena and the scientific and historical methods of dealing with them can therefore be set forth as follows:

Levels	Formation of Processes	Depiction of Phenomena
Superorganic Phenomena	Social Psychology	Cultural History
Mental Organic Phenomena	Psychology	Biographic History
Vital Organic Phenomena	Physiology	Natural History
Organic Phenomena	Physics, Chemistry	Astronomy, Geology

Every human situation has environmental, organic, social, and cultural dimensions. When we concentrate on a personality or some such limited area, all these factors are seen as many dimensions "radiating" from the point under observation. But when we approach larger areas and trace large historic patterns or their inter-relations, the aspects so harmonized appear as superimposed layers or levels.

The social level is distinguished from the cultural level because cultural and social phenomena are thoroughly distinct though they coexist in man. Many kinds of insects lead an intensive socialized existence. But they do not manifest even the rudiments of culture. Culture is therefore the top level of the hierarchy of phenomena. There may be a level higher than the cultural level. Kroeber's views regarding this are: "Personally, I would not have the glimmering of a suspicion as to what a level or organization higher than that of culture might be like. Yet a future generation may see more clearly."[3] This higher level may have found a different kind of expression in philosophy, religion, and the arts. But the anthropologists do not wish to investigate levels which may be connected with unknown or *unmapped levels of consciousness*.

There are two totally separate evolutions—that of the organic level and that of the social level. The social level is not a link in a chain but a leap to another plane like the first occurrence of life in a lifeless universe. Culture is divisible into three levels which Kroeber has called the levels of reality culture, social culture, and value culture. A better name for reality culture is what Kroeber himself suggested earlier: subsistence culture. Reality culture is diffusional and accumulative. A new generation can take it up where the other left it. Social culture is neither specifically accumulative nor specifically creative. Value culture, however, is ever creative.

The components of culture have, therefore, to be analyzed at these three levels. At the level of subsistence culture, we can include the achievements under applied science or technology, the devices, instruments and skills directed to the achievement of goals. Here come the useful arts like pottery and weaving. Kroeber even regards medicine and engineering as useful arts in spite of the scientific processes that they employ, because it is the ultimate practical purposes demanding it that determine whether a subject is a science or art.

The level of social existence is concerned with social structure and action— the economic systems of both production and distribution, the political system of governance (State), the structure of family, clan, tribe, community or any other social groupings, race, in fact, the whole area of human social relationships.

The third level of value culture or "fine" or "creative" culture includes achievements under the fine arts, philosophy, religion, traditions, codes and customs, and play activities. Even scientific activity, when it is purely intellectual and non-utilitarian, belongs here. So do Mathematics and Logic.

[3]*Ibid.*, p. 124.

The classification accepted above should not be regarded as an absolute one. It is only a conceptual axis within one area which is useful for clear understanding. But it is bound to be capricious if it is pushed too far.

Thus, for example, language is a fourth component of culture which serves the three levels referred to above, but its mechanism is not an end in itself. The fifth component is ethics or morality and law. It is rooted in values which have been included under the third level. But it functions as the basic regulator at the second or social level, particularly when it is expressed as law.

The sixth component of culture is fashion. It is dedicated to values, but its values are trivial and ever-changing, though they have considerable social significance.

It will be seen, therefore, that the study of culture, which the anthropologists have adopted as their main concern, demands familiarity with a number of sciences. It has to gather its materials through a number of auxiliary sciences such as ceramics, archaeology, ethnology, and technology at the first level; economics, sociology and political science at the second level; philosophy, aesthetics, religion and personality psychology at the third level; and other sciences like linguistics and geography, which, in a way, are concerned with all these levels. It is only when we face human activity comprehensively, from all these angles, that we arrive at an integrated concept of the culture of any group of people.

It is impossible to say positively what leads to the configuration of the great cultures of the world. Spengler thinks that, at the bottom of the formation of a great civilization, lies immanent predestination. On the other hand, Toynbee thinks that the causal agent is the moral free will of man asserting itself during certain epochs and leading to great achievement. Sorokin thinks that the rise and fall of civilizations is due to the oscillation between sensate and ideational proclivities. It is difficult to say how a great civilization, like the Graeco-Roman or the ancient Indian, was born. What we can do is to study them in depth and have a total view of what they stood for. It is not as though the peak values of any cultural system were abosrbed by all human beings who were responsible for its emergence and growth. The diffusion of a system of cultural values among its own people may be studied as one of the interesting problems connected with the system itself.

Index